Sects & Sectarianism

Also by Bhikkhu Sujato through Santipada

A History of Mindfulness
How tranquillity worsted insight in the Pali canon

Beginnings
There comes a time when the world ends...

Bhikkhuni Vinaya Studies
Research & reflections on monastic discipline for Buddhist nuns

A Swift Pair of Messengers
Calm and insight in the Buddha's words

Dreams of Bhaddā
Sex. Murder. Betrayal. Enlightenment. The story of a Buddhist nun.

White Bones Red Rot Black Snakes
A Buddhist mythology of the feminine

SANTIPADA is a non-profit Buddhist publisher. These and many other works are available in a variety of paper and digital formats.

http://santipada.org

Sects & Sectarianism

The origins of Buddhist schools

BHIKKHU SUJATO

SANTIPADA

SANTIPADA
Buddhism as if life matters

Originally published by The Corporate Body of the Buddha Education Foundation, Taiwan, 2007.
This revised edition published in 2012 by Santipada.
Printed and distributed by Lulu.com.

ISBN: 978-1-921842-06-1

Typeset in Gentium using LuaLaTeX.

Cover image kindly made available by Kirk Dunne:
http://kirkdunne.com/blog/?attachment_id=135

The Sangha of bhikkhus and bhikkhunis has been made unified.

As long as my children and grandchildren shall live, and as long as the sun and the moon shall shine, any bhikkhu or bhikkhuni who divides the Sangha shall be made to wear white clothes and dwell outside the monasteries.

What it is my wish?

That the unity of the Sangha should last a long time.

—King Aśoka, Minor Pillar Edict, Sāñchī

Contents

Sectarian Views on the Schools

Mahāsaṅghika Śāriputraparipṛcchā

The Mahāsaṅghika school diligently study the collected Suttas and teach the true meaning, because they are the source and the center. They wear yellow robes.

The Dharmaguptaka school master the flavor of the true way. They are guides for the benefit of all. Their way of expression is special. They wear red robes.

The Sarvāstivāda school quickly gain unobstructed knowledge, for the Dhamma is their guide. They wear black robes.

The Kaśyapīya school are diligent and energetic in guarding sentient beings. They wear magnolia robes.

The Mahīśāsaka school practice jhana, and penetrate deeply. They wear blue robes.

(T24, № 1465, p. 900, c12–18)

Theravāda Dīpavaṁsa

These 17 sects are schismatic,
only one sect is non-schismatic.

With the non-schismatic sect,
there are eighteen in all.

Like a great banyan tree,
the Theravāda is supreme,

The Dispensation of the Conqueror,
complete, without lack or excess.

The other sects arose
like thorns on the tree.

(Dīpavaṁsa 4.90–91)

FOREWORD

THESE TWO QUOTES, each from essential texts, highlight two radically different perspectives on the Buddhist schisms.[1] Are we to see the emerging schools as a corruption of an originally pure unity, or as unique unfoldings of the potential of the Dhamma? My own belief is that both of these perspectives are likely to contain some truth, and yet neither of them contains the whole truth.

2 If we reflect on the issues that divided the schools, we find much that is reminiscent of contemporary Buddhist dialogue. It is a shame that the complex and profound history of Buddhist thought is reduced to the facile dismissal of other schools simply because they disagree with the interpretation of one's own chosen party. As much as we would like to imagine that all the answers are wrapped up, the nature of philosophy is such that the basic issues that generated schools of thought remain, and reappear in varied guises in discussions within the school itself.

3 For example, the Mahāsaṅghika's basic thesis was the transcendental nature of the Buddha. We might regard some of the extremes of this view with amusement—such as the idea that dirt never clings to the Buddha's body, but he washes it in conformity with everyday usage—but it address a genuine Buddhist concern: how do we conceive of the nature of Buddhahood, so intensely human yet so totally beyond our lives of anxiety and fear? This is a live issue within Theravāda Buddhism even today. While the official (read 'rationalist, modernist, middle class') position is that

[1] The Śāriputraparipṛcchā's claims about the robe colors of the various schools need not be taken literally.

the Buddha was 'just' a perfected human, the devotional perspective of ordinary Theravādins sees him as something quite other.

4 Similarly, the Sarvāstivādins taught a philosophical realism that tended to treat external objects as 'existing' in and of themselves, so that even an abstract relation like 'possession' comes to be considered as a real substance. This comes across as naïve, but in shaping their philosophy they show a consciousness of a fundamental problem of metaphysics: if we allow the 'existence' of one thing it becomes difficult to deny the existence of everything. So the Sarvāstivādins considered that the past and the future 'exist' in exactly the same sense as the present. The Sarvāstivādins were perfectly aware that this appeared to flaunt the fundamental Buddhist axiom of impermanence. But they were trying to explain impermanence based not on ontology, but on causal efficacy: the present 'exists' just as the past and future 'exist', but the present is distinguished in that it is operative or functional. To invoke a modern analogy, compare this with the buttons on the word processing document I'm typing; they all 'exist', but only become operative when I hover the cursor above them: that moment is the 'present'. We may question the exact formulation of this idea, but we should do so as the Sarvāstivādins themselves did, that is, within a Buddhist context, seeking the best way to articulate Buddhist truths. We would need to address the same question faced by the Sarvāstivādins: if all is impermanent, what is there that connects the past, future, and present? This question is much more than an abstract musing. In a devotional religion like Buddhism, it is crucial in forming our emotional attitude towards our beloved Teacher, so present in our consciousness, yet so remote in time. Theravādins, despite the stern official doctrine of radical momentariness, still popularly treat the Buddha as somehow still existing, resulting in an uneasy dichotomy between the official and the popular perspectives. The Sarvāstivādin approach would allow a less fractured understanding throughout the community, which might be one reason behind its extraordinary success in ancient India.

5 As another example, the Puggalavādins took their stand on the thesis that there exists a 'person' who is neither identical with nor separate from the five aggregates that make up our empirical reality. This 'person' is indescribable, but is not the 'self' of the non-Buddhist theorists. It is this

'person' which experiences the fruit of kamma and which attains liberation. The Puggalavādins were not blind to the difficulties in reconciling this theory with the teaching of 'not-self'. Quite the opposite; their main philosophical efforts went into a sophisticated articulation of how the 'person' was in fact the correct understanding of 'not-self'. Once more, this is a key issue in modern Buddhist dialogue. How do we reconcile the 'atomic' reality of our empirical experience with the undeniable sense of personal identity? This problem is especially acute in the relation between Buddhist and psychological thought. Much of psychology is concerned with building a coherent and integrated 'self', a project that is anathema to a literal interpretation of traditional Buddhism. But the psychological approach has developed in response to a genuine problem, the fractured and alienated modern psyche. This is a very different context to what the Buddha was facing when he critiqued Brahmanical or Jainist theories of a permanent and enduring essence that survived death. As we develop our modern responses to such questions, it would seem sensible to recognize that we are not the first generation to grapple with how to apply Buddhism in a historical context far removed from the Buddha's own.

6 In pursuing the historical inquiry throughout this work, then, I take it for granted that the various sects all attempted to articulate and practice sincerely the Buddha's teachings. When examined closely, the doctrines of the schools cannot be explained away as simplistic errors or alien infiltrations or deliberate corruptions. It would then follow that more sympathetic and gentle perspectives on the schools are likely to be more objective than bitterly partisan accounts.

7 It seems to me that far too much weight has been ascribed to the Dīpavaṁsa, the earliest Sri Lankan chronicle. This version of events, despite straining credibility in almost every respect, continues to exert a powerful influence on the Theravādin sense of communal identity. The fact that some modern scholars have treated it favourably only reinforces this tendency.

8 The research contained in this work was primarily inspired by my involvement in the reformation of the bhikkhuni order within Theravāda. While we will only glance upon this issue here, one of the central questions in the revival of the bhikkhuni lineage from the Theravādin perspective is

the validity of ordination lineages in other schools. The traditional Theravādin view has it that the bhikkhunis in existence today are 'Mahāyāna'. Mahāyāna, it is claimed, is descended from the Mahāsaṅghikas, and the Dīpavaṁsa asserts that the Mahāsaṅghikas are none other than the 'evil' Vajjiputtakas, who advocated the use of money by monks, and who were defeated at the Second Council, but who later reformed and made a new recitation. Hence the Mahāyāna is representative of a tradition whose fundamental principle was to encourage laxity in Vinaya. They are 'schismatic' and it is impossible to accept them as part of the same communion.

9 This view, ultimately traced to the Dīpavaṁsa, underlies the position taken by many mainstream Theravādins today. I intend to show how the Dīpavaṁsa's position is incoherent and implausible, and that a more reasonable depiction of the origins of Buddhist schools can be constructed from a sympathetic reading of all the sources.

10 Recently I was at a meeting where these issues were discussed. A Vietnamese monk acknowledged his lineage from the Dharmaguptaka Vinaya; a Tibetan monk noted his heritage from the Mūlasarvāstivāda Vinaya; but the Theravādins continued to speak as if they were simply 'Mahāyāna'. This situation, regrettable though it is, is understandable since most Theravādins have never heard of 'Dharmagupta' or 'Mūlasarvāstivāda'. Once the 17 schools had been dismissed as 'schismatic' and 'thorns' by the Dīpavaṁsa, and their doctrines had been refuted by the Kathāvatthu, there was no need to be informed about the other schools.

11 But there has never been a distinctively 'Mahāyāna' Vinaya or ordination lineage. Rather, some bhikkhus and bhikkhunis, having ordained in one of the lineages of the early schools, study and practice the texts and ethical ideals known as 'Mahāyāna'. This was, so far as we can tell, the case in ancient India and it remains the case today. Today, the bhikkhus and bhikkhunis of the East Asian traditions follow the Vinaya of the Dharmaguptaka school, while the Central Asian traditions follow the Mūlasarvāstivāda. There is, therefore, no such thing as a 'Mahāyāna' bhikkhu or bhikkhuni from the Vinaya point of view. The Vinayas themselves are silent on the question of the sects. If we wish to understand the relationship between the existing Sanghas of the various schools, then, we must investigate the relationships between the early schools of Buddhism from whom the Vinayas and ordination lineages derive.

12 One way of doing this is to examine the origins of the schools in question. Here we enter into the swirling and uncertain world of mythology, where interpretation reigns sovereign, and sectarian bias is not merely expected, but is the driving motivation. Given the contradictory, incomplete, and doubtful nature of the literary sources it is unclear whether we can expect to find even a glimmer of truth. But our surest evidence derives from the happy coincidence of the historical/mythic accounts and archeological findings, and it is here that we begin our search.

13 I would like to offer a more realistic picture of sectarian formation to practicing Buddhists. Though I use the methods and results of modern scholarship, I do not wish to speak to a purely academic audience. I hope there are some Buddhists willing to take the time to examine history a little more carefully, and not just to accept the polemics of their school based on ancient sectarian rivalries.

14 It would have been nice if I could have digested the work of modern researchers and simply presented that in a palatable form. But there are many of the findings of the moderns that are as unacceptable as the traditions of the schools. It seems to me that much modern work, while it has accomplished a great deal, is hampered by the problems that bedevil Buddhist studies in general: uncritical acceptance of textual evidence over archaeological findings; bias in favour of either the southern or northern traditions; reliance on inaccurate or mistaken readings from secondary works and translations; simplistic and unrealistic notions of religious life in general and monastic life in particular; little knowledge of the Vinaya; backreading of later situations into earlier times; and perhaps most importantly, an ignorance of myth, so that 'historical' information is divorced from the mythic context that gave it meaning.

15 Extraordinary thanks are due to Bhikkhuni Samacittā for her help in the Chinese translations, and Bhikkhu Santidhammo helping me understand the nature of schism and community. Thanks are also due to Bhikkhu Bodhi, who gave his time to reading my work and offering his comments. Marcus Bingenheimer, Bhikkhuni Thubten Chodren, Rod Bucknell, Bhikkhuni Chi Kwang Sunim, Bhikkhuni Jampa Tsedron, Terry Waugh, Mark Allon,

Bhikkhuni Sudhamma, and many others have offered feedback and support. I would also like to extend my appreciation to the donors who have supported my monk's life, offering me what I needed make this work possible: *sādhu, sādhu, anumodāmi*!

16 While researching I have investigated several areas that are tangential to the main argument of the book. In some cases these are mere technical remarks, while others critique certain specific interpretations of relevant issues, and still others are sketches toward further study. These essays, together with the text of the current book, may be found at:

http://sectsandsectarianism.santipada.org

ABSTRACT

THE CONCEPT OF A 'SCHOOL' that has been evolving in my mind as I pursue this work has something to do with the notion of a 'distinct totality': a group of Sangha who see themselves as in some sense distinct from other Sangha, and who view their own system as complete, adequate for a full spiritual life. This would involve a textual tradition, devotional centres, lineage of masters, institutional support, etc. When these factors are there to a sufficient degree for a particular portion of the Sangha to agree that they themselves constitute such a 'distinct totality', we can speak of a school.

2 Let us consider the main evidence for sectarian formation, dividing our sources into two groups, those before and those after the Common Era (about 400–500 AN), and see where such a distinct totality can be observed. Within each group I shall consider the archeological evidence first, as that can clearly be fixed in time. The dates of all of the textual sources are questionable, and most of them probably straddle our divide. Nevertheless, I try to assign a place as best I can.

0.1 The Early Period (BCE)

3 Here our main sources are the archaeological evidence of the Aśokan inscriptions and the Vedisa stupas and inscriptions, the doxographical literature (Kathāvatthu and Vijñānakāya), and the Sinhalese Vinaya Commentary (which by its definite links with the archaeological evidence is proved to have roots in this period). We might also include the Aśoka legends which, while lacking such distinct archaeological confirmation as the

Vinaya Commentary, nevertheless may have at least some origins in this period.

4 The Aśokan inscriptions do not mention any schools or any explicit occurrence of schism. When the edicts say the Sangha has been 'made unified', this suggests that there has been some conflict, but it falls short of establishing that a schism had occurred. In any case, even if there had been a schism, the edicts assert that it had been resolved. Nor do the Aśokan edicts mention any doctrines, texts, or anything else that might even hint at the existence of schools. The main sect-formative factor at work here would appear to be the geographical spread of the Sangha, which was to become a powerful force in the evolution of distinct sectarian identities.

5 The inscriptions on reliquaries retrieved from the stupas in Vedisa mention several sectarian-formative factors, such as local saints, local institutions, and the name Hemavata, which at least at some time was taken to be the name of a school. But there is no clear and definitive evidence for the existence of a school. Hemavata may be purely a geographical term here. As Cousins observes, no unambiguous evidence for any Hemavata texts has survived, so the status of this school is doubtful in any case. The emergence of a local identity is a natural progression from the geographical spread under Aśoka, and we have no evidence that the Vedisa community saw itself as distinct from other Buddhist communities.

6 The doxographical literature likewise shows sectarian-formative factors, particularly the articulation of controversial doctrines that characterized certain schools. But there is no explicit acknowledgement of the existence of schools, with the sole exception of the mention of the Puggalavāda in the Vijñānakāya.

7 The Sinhalese Vinaya Commentary was finalized much later, but there is definite archaeological evidence that proves the relevant portions must stem from genuine historical records. This is particularly true in the case of the Sudassanavinayavibhāsā, which was evidently taken to China and translated from a text predating Buddhaghosa's revision of the commentaries in the the 5th century CE. This details an extensive account of the period in question, and finds no reason to mention even in passing the existence of any schools.

8 Likewise the Aśokavadāna, Aśokarājasūtra, Divyavadāna, etc., give many elaborate stories of Aśoka without involving the schools. Of course these legendary works were much augmented over time, but if anything this strengthens our argument: since these texts were doubtless finalized in the sectarian period, there must have been a temptation to explicitly associate Aśoka with their own school. But this was not done.

9 Summing up this period, there is no evidence unambiguously belonging to the early period that mentions or implies the existence of schools. We find only the mention of various forces that lead to sectarian formation, never to the actual schools that resulted from these forces. This remains true even if we allow texts that are actually finalized later, but which probably have roots in this period.

0.2 The Middle Period (CE)

10 For this period our primary sources are the inscriptional evidence, the various schism accounts, and the *śāstra*/commentarial literature.

11 The inscriptions, starting in Mathura around 100 CE, regularly mention the names of schools.

12 The *śāstras* (e.g. Abhidharmakośa, etc.) and commentaries (e.g. Kathāvatthu-aṭṭhakathā, Mahāvibhāṣā, etc.) regularly mention schools by name, and discuss their doctrines. The textual sources agree fairly well with each other, and also with the inscriptions.

13 The schism accounts again mention similar names and sometimes similar doctrines as the other sources.

14 It is the schism accounts we must discuss in more detail, as they are the main sources from which the idea of an early schism was derived. The main four texts are closely related and must hark back to the same original in certain respects. But in the form we have them today they represent the perspectives of the four main groups of schools. Certain other lists are disregarded here (such as Bhavya I & II) but I believe they will not change matters significantly. These four main texts are the Śāriputraparipṛcchā (Mahāsaṅghika); Vasumitra's Samayabhedoparacanacakra (Sarvāstivāda: this should be interpreted together with the Mahāvibhāṣā), the Dīpavaṁsa (Mahāvihāra/Vibhajjavāda/Sthavira), and Bhavya III (Puggalavāda).

15 These accounts can be further divided into two pairs by date. The Sāriputraparipṛcchā and Vasumitra are earlier, probably dating around 200 CE. The Dīpavaṁsa and Bhavya III are more like 400 CE (although the text of Bhavya III is later still, 600+ CE).

16 The Śāriputraparipṛcchā, which is the earliest or second-earliest of the schism accounts, stems from the Mahāsaṅghika. This account, which attributes the schism to an attempt on the part of the Sthaviras to expand the ancient Vinaya, dates the schism about a century after Aśoka. As we have seen, this is in perfect accord with all the inscriptural evidence, and with all the early textual evidence. It has been discounted by scholars who have asserted the text is corrupt and chronologically confused. However, a close examination of the text does not support this. The text is, admittedly, a poor and difficult translation, but the chronology of the period in question fits coherently into an overall narrative. The schism cannot be arbitrarily moved back before Aśoka without destroying this context. Indeed, one of the main purposes of the narrative is to claim the mythic authority of Upagupta, Aśoka's teacher, for the Mahāsaṅghika school.

17 Vasumitra places the schism at the time of Aśoka, which for his short chronology is 100+ AN. This version, which attributes the schism to a dispute on the 'five theses' at Pāṭaliputta, is closely related to the Mahāvibhāṣā and Bhavya III. But we note that, while these three sources describe the same event, only Vasumitra connects this explicitly with Aśoka. Due to different ways of counting the years between the Buddha and Aśoka, the dating is hoplessly confused: Vasumitra places the events at Aśoka, which it says is 100+ AN; Bhavya III places the same events *before* Aśoka, but the date is 137 AN. The Mahāvibhāṣā does not name the king, so provides no support for any particular dating. In addition, the story, which is an outrageously polemical attack on 'Mahādeva', is only found in the larger and presumably later Mahāvibhāṣā, which dates at least half a millenium after the event. From the Mahāvibhāṣā we can see how the Sarvāstivāda school used these events to develop a distinctive mythos explaining how they came to be established in Kaśmīr. This would provide ample motivation for the Sarvāstivādins to associate the schism with Aśoka, regardless of any actual historical facts.

18 The Dīpavaṁsa was compiled shortly before Buddhaghosa, and is therefore significantly later than the Śāriputraparipṛcchā or Vasumitra. Dating 700 years after the events, it is the first text that claims that the schism was pre-Aśokan, in fact just after the Second Council in 100 AN. The account of the schisms has been inserted from a Vasumitra-style text. However, the cause of the schism (textual corruption), the date, and the place (Vesālī) are all completely different. It has been crudely interpolated into a retelling of the story of the Councils otherwise preserved in the Sinhala Vinaya Commentaries. There is no need to assume that the original context of the interpolated schism account placed the events in this particular historical context; on the contrary, the setting is obviously incongruous. The Dīpavaṁsa's dating of the schism just after the Second Council was probably an invention of the author(s) of the Dīpavaṁsa itself, whose aim was to establish an exclusivist mythos for the Mahāvihāra. The historical credibility of this account approaches zero.

19 Finally, like the Dīpavaṁsa, Bhavya III places the schism before Aśoka. But the events have nothing to do with the account of the Dīpavaṁsa. Rather it attributes the schism to the 'five theses' as does Vasumitra, with dating inconsistencies as I mention above. The lack of mythic context makes this account harder to assess, but no doubt it was pressed into service to authorize the Puggalavāda school. We note that it is the two latest sources (Bhavya III and Dīpavaṁsa) that place the schism pre-Aśoka. It seems that the schism date is gradually getting earlier, a natural feature of the mythic process.

20 To summarize this period, then, we have consistent, clear evidence of the Buddhist schools dating from the middle period (post-CE). In all of our accounts of Buddhism of this period, the existence and basic nature of the schools is taken for granted and constitutes an essential component. The agreement of the sources as far as the names of the schools, their interrelationships, and their distinctive doctrines is, all things considered, reasonably high, as we would expect since they are describing contemporary conditions. But their accounts of the origins of the schisms, already in the far distant past from their own perspective, are a mass of contradictions. In the three schism accounts that supply sufficient information (Śāriputraparipṛcchā, Vasumitra/Mahāvibhāṣā, Dīpavaṁsa), the primary

function of the accounts was not to record history but to authorize their own school. I believe this provides sufficient reason to explain how the schools came up with their various dating systems.

21 Of course, this does not prove that the dates in these texts are all wrong. It is quite possible and in fact very common to construct a mythology out of real events. But given the evident contradictions I think it is sheer naïvity to use the dates given in these texts to reach any simple historical conclusions. Like all myths, they are describing the situation in their own time (a situation of sectarian Buddhism) and backdating that in search of archaic authorization.

0.3 Comparing pre-CE & post-CE evidence

22 Despite the complexities of the situation, which any account including my own must inevitably distort by simplifying, the overall pattern is remarkably consistent. All the evidence of the early period (pre-CE) seems to be quite happy to talk about Buddhism with no mention of the schools. In stark contrast, in the middle period (post-CE) material the existence of the schools is inherent in how Buddhism is conceived. The textual and archaeological evidence is in good agreement here.

23 I conclude that various separative forces gathered momentum through the early period and manifested in the emergence of 'schools' towards the end of the early period, as depicted in the Śāriputraparipṛcchā (and various Chinese and Tibetan works). As the question of sectarian identity became more conscious, mythic accounts of the schisms emerged in the middle period.

0.4 The Mahāvihāravāsins

24 To find a more realistic description of how the schools may have arisen we shall have to look elsewhere. One of the fullest accounts of the origination of any school is found in the Sinhalese Vinaya Commentary, which exists in a Pali version the Samantapāsādikā, and an ancient Chinese translation the Sudassanavinayavibhāsā (T24 善見律毘婆沙 Shan-Jian-Lu-Pi-Po-Sha). The Sinhalese Vinaya Commentary recounts several decisive events

that took place in the time of Aśoka. There was a conflict in the Sangha that was resolved by the expulsion of corrupt monks by Aśoka together with the Elder Moggaliputtatissa, following which the 'Third Council' was held to reaffirm communal identity. Subsequently Moggaliputtatissa organized the sending out of 'missionaries' to various parts of India. The main purpose of this narrative is to establish the credentials of the Sinhalese school.

25 Today we call this school 'Theravāda', but this name invites various forms of confusion. In particular it is a mistake to identify this school with the 'Sthaviras' who split from the Mahāsaṅghikas at the first schism. Rather, the Mahāvihāravāsins are just one branch of the Sthaviras who became established in Sri Lanka with their headquarters at the Mahāvihāra in Anuradhapura. In their own texts they refer to themselves as the Mahāvihāravāsins ('Dwellers in the Great Monastery') and I will adopt this term. It should be noted that when I refer to texts of this school this does not imply that the school necessarily created the texts in question; I simply mean the texts 'as accepted by' or 'as passed down by' the Mahāvihāra. In some cases these texts were authored by the school, but many of them are shared in common with other schools, with varying degrees of editorial differences.

26 There are two major pieces of inscriptional evidence that derive from the early period of Indian Buddhism: the Aśokan edicts and the reliquaries at Vedisa. Strikingly, both of these confirm the evidence found in Sinhalese Vinaya Commentary. The Vedisa inscriptions mention the names of several monks who the Sinhalese Vinaya Commentary says were sent as missionaries to the Himalaya soon after the 'Third Council'. And Aśoka's so-called 'schism edicts' (which actually state that the Sangha is unified, not schismatic!) mention an expulsion of corrupt bhikkhus, which many scholars have identified with the events prior to the 'Third Council'. We should also note that Moggaliputtatissa's sending out of missionaries has often been compared with Aśoka's sending out of Dhamma-ministers; and that the Sri Lankan archaeological record is in general agreement with the picture of the missions. These two evidences, while not decisive, provide further points of agreement between the Sinhalese Vinaya Commentary and the archaeological record. This correspondence between epigraphic

and textual evidence encourages us to take the missions account of the Sinhalese Vinaya Commentary seriously as a source for the origins of the schools.

27 The missions account describes how the Sinhalese school was established by Aśoka's son Mahinda and his daughter the bhikkhuni Saṅghamittā. Several other teachers are described as being sent out to different places. While many of these missions cannot be confirmed, Frauwallner and others have shown that there is a general pattern of plausibility in the account.

28 In the current context of the revival of the bhikkhuni lineage in Theravāda, it is worth remembering the mission of Soṇa and Uttara to Suvaṇṇabhūmi, which is believed by Burmese to refer to Burma, and by Thais to refer to Thailand. This mission, which to this day forms a crucial narrative of self-identity for Buddhists in these regions, was said to result in the ordination of 1500 women. Thus bhikkhuni ordination is intrinsic to Southeast Asian Buddhism from the beginning.

0.5 The Dharmaguptakas

29 One of the other missionaries was Yonaka Dhammarakkhita. He was, as his name indicates, a Greek monk, native of 'Alasanda' (Alexandria). One of the major figures in the missions narrative, he features in the Pali tradition as a master of psychic powers as well as an expert on Abhidhamma. He went to the Greek occupied areas in the west of India. Long ago Pryzluski, followed by Frauwallner, suggested that Dhammarakkhita be identified with the founder of the Dharmaguptaka school, since *dhammarakkhita* and *dhammagutta* have identical meaning. Since that time two pieces of evidence have come to light that make this suggestion highly plausible. One is the positive identication of very early manuscripts belonging to the Dharmaguptakas in the Gandhāra region, exactly where we expect to find Yonaka Dhammarakkhita. The second is that his name in the Sudassanavinayavibhāsā (the Chinese version of the Sinhalese Vinaya commentary) is evidently 'Dharmagutta' rather than 'Dhammarakkhita'. We also note that several texts say that the Dharmaguptaka was started by a certain 'Moggallāna'. While this is traditionally identified with the great disciple of that name, I think it is more reasonable to see this as a reference to

Moggaliputtatissa, the patriarch of the Third Council, who is also regarded by the Mahāvihāravāsins as their founder. We are thus perfectly justified as seeing the Mahāvihāravāsins and the Dharmaguptakas, not as warring schismatic parties, but as long lost brothers parted only by the accidents of history and the tyranny of distance.

0.6 The Mūlasarvāstivādins

30 With regard to the third of our schools, the Mūlasarvāstivādins, the history is decidedly murky. In my opinion the most persuasive theory for the origin of this school was again provided by Frauwallner, who argued that they were originally based in Mathura. This would align this school closely with the famous arahants of Mathura: Śāṇavāsin and Upagupta. Śāṇavāsin features as a revered Elder and Vinaya master in the Vinaya accounts of the Second Council. He is said to have established a major forest monastery, which is called Urumuṇḍa in the northern sources and Ahogaṅga in the Pali.

31 Later on, it was to this very monastery that Moggaliputtatissa resorted for retreat. The spiritual power Moggaliputtatissa derived from his time in Śāṇavāsin's forest monastery was decisive in convincing Aśoka to entrust him with the task of purifying the Saṅgha and organizing the missions. Thus the establishment of the Mahāvihāravāsin and Dharmaguptaka is closely associated with the Śāṇavāsin lineage. It is even possible that Soṇaka, the preceptor of Moggaliputtatissa's preceptor, is simply a misspelling for Śāṇaka(-vāsin), in which case the Mahāvihāravāsin ordination lineage is directly descended from Śāṇavāsin and the forest tradition of Mathura.

32 If Frauwallner's theory of the distinct Mathuran origins of the Mūlasarvāstivāda school is found to be incorrect, then it would seem inevitable that we should seek the origins of this school as somehow related to the Sarvāstivādins of Kaśmīr. Buddhism was brought to Kaśmīr by one of the other Aśokan missionaries, Majjhantika. After serving as Mahinda's ordination teacher in Pāṭaliputra, he went to Kaśmir and established the school later known as the Sarvāstivāda. This account associating Majjhantika and

Mahinda agrees with the versions of the northern schools (except they generally place the date earlier).

33 In conclusion, we find that there is no evidence whatsoever of the origination of schools due to 'schism' in the narrowly defined sense required by the Vinaya. The emergence of monastic communities as 'distinct totalities' probably occurred gradually after the Aśokan period as a natural consequence of geographical dispersion and consequent differentiation. The accounts of the origins of the schools that we possess today are responses to events at the time the accounts were written, not genuine historical records. In the normal mythic manner, contemporary conflicts shaped how the past is imagined, motivated by the need for archaic authorization.

Chapter 1

THE 'UNITY EDICTS'

AŚOKA PUBLISHED EDICTS in three places concerning the Sangha, which have become known as the 'Schism Edicts'. This is a misnomer, and itself was probably influenced by the expectations of modern scholars that in Aśoka's time the Sangha was already fragmented. The edicts depict a state of unity in the Sangha, not a state of schism.

2 The three tantalizingly brief inscriptions are found on the 'Minor Pillar Edicts' of Sarnath, Sāñchī, and Kosambi in varying states of disrepair, strung along the route between Pāṭaliputta, Aśoka's capital, to Avanti and Vedisa. These are all within the older realm of Buddhism.

3 The edicts instruct Aśoka's ministers that, now that the Sangha has been made united,[1] any bhikkhu or bhikkhuni who divides the Sangha should be made to wear lay clothes and dwell apart. The Sāñchī edict adds that this united Sangha, of both bhikkhus and bhikkhunis, should not be divided 'as long as my sons and grandsons shall rule, and the sun and moon shall shine, for it is my wish that the united Sangha should remain for a long time'.[2] The Sarnath edict adds that a copy of this edict is to be made available for the lay devotees, who should review this message each fortnightly *uposatha*.

4 The statement that the Sangha has been 'made unified' suggests an actual, not a theoretical event, to which these Edicts respond by warning

---

[1] Sāñchī: *[Saṁ](ghe)e*[sa]*mag(e) kate*; Kosambi: *(sa)ma(ge)* kate* saṁghas[i].*

[2] *Ichā hi me kiṁ-ti saṁghe samage cilathitīke siyā.*

of the grave consequences of schismatic conduct. The fact that the Edicts are found in several places suggests that the tendencies to schism were widespread, and, if the Edicts were implemented, there may have been several episodes. The Sarnath Edict starts with a partially defaced reading: *pāṭa[liput]* ..., which seems to be referring to Pāṭaliputta. This suggests that, as one might expect, the schismatic forces were at work in the capital, probably centred there. If this is so, then Aśoka's instructions to his ministers would, as usual, be for them to follow his personal example. Thus we could think of a central crisis in the capital dealt with by Aśoka personally, and possibly several lesser repercussions throughout the realm, dealt with by the ministers.

5 There is no precedent in Vinaya for a secular ruler to interfere in this way in the Sangha's operations. While the Vinaya envisages a Sangha that is competent to look after its own affairs, with a tacit assumption that the governing powers will provide general support, now we have a ruler directly imposing his will on the Sangha. Perhaps the most surprising thing is that the Sangha seems to have welcomed this interference. This could only be explained if the problem was a genuine one, which the Sangha was unable to deal with using its normal procedures (*saṅghakamma*). Sangha procedures almost always require consensus, and so they assume a high degree of sincerity and co-operativeness. This is how the dispute was solved at the Second Council. But if the problematic individuals disrupt the very functioning of *saṅghakamma*, the Sangha is powerless.

1.1 Schism & unity

6 To understand the Unity Edicts, we must first consider the nature of schism and unity. In Buddhism, the original and archetypical schismatic is the Buddha's wicked cousin Devadatta, the Judas or Set of Buddhism. His story is too long and too well known to repeat here.[3] All stories of schism have Devadatta in the back of their mind, and all tellers of those stories are struggling to balance two forces: to justify and authorize their

[3] A typical popular account of Devadatta's story at http://www.tipitaka.net/pali/ebooks/pageload.php?book=0003&page=17. An alternative view in RAY.

own separate school, while at the same time strenuously avoiding any suggestion that they are following in Devadatta's footprints.

7 This is apparent in the Unity Edicts, for the terminology Aśoka uses echoes exactly that of the famous passage where the Buddha warns Devadatta that one who divides a unified Sangha will suffer in hell for an aeon, whereas one who 'makes unified a divided Sangha'[4] will rejoice in heaven for an aeon. This phrasing occurs repeatedly in the passages that follow.[5] When the Sangha, having been divided on one of these issues, holds separate *uposatha*, *pavāraṇā* or *saṅghakamma*, a schism results.[6]

8 This parallels the meaning of schism given in my Oxford Reference Dictionary: 'The separation of a Church into two Churches or the secession of a group owing to doctrinal, disciplinary, etc., differences.' It will be one of our tasks to determine whether all of the historical divisions of Buddhism into different schools, or indeed any of them, were schisms in this sense.

9 Contemporary discussion of this question has emphasized two rather different forms of schism. Bechert uses the terminology of *saṅghabheda* to refer to a split of an individual community, and *nikāyabheda* to refer to the process of school formation. Sasaki uses *kammabheda* and *cakkabheda* to make a similar distinction: *kammabheda* occurs when two groups hold *uposatha* separately within the same boundary, while *cakkabheda* refers to the splitting of the religious community on doctrinal grounds.[7] The key point in these distinction is that the formation of schools does not necessarily imply a *saṅghabheda*. To clarify this point let us look more closely at the Vinaya passages, starting with the Pali.

---

4 Pali Vinaya 2.198: *Saṅghaṁ samaggaṁ karoti.*

5 Incidentally, these passages also clarify that, contrary to popular opinion, it is not the case that all schisms entail that the schismatic will be doomed to hell for an aeon. This only applies if one deliberately and maliciously divides the Sangha, declaring Dhamma to be not-Dhamma, Vinaya to be not-Vinaya, etc., in the manner of Devadatta.

6 Pali Vinaya 2.204. *Uposatha* is the fortnightly recitation of the monastic code; *pavāraṇā* is the mutual invitation for admonition at the end of the yearly rains retreat; *saṅghakamma* is a general term for such formal 'acts of the Sangha', including ordination (*upasampadā*).

7 My response to Sasaki is at http://sectsandsectarianism/santipada.org/sasakiandschism. In brief, I argue that the historical shift from *cakrabheda* to *karmabheda* is not sufficiently established by Sasaki's evidence, and would rather see these two as representing the informal and formal aspects of the same process: *karmabheda* is the legal juncture at which *cakrabheda* is complete.

10 Devadatta's conduct occasioned the laying down of a *saṅghādisesa* rule prohibiting the deliberate agitation for schism. The rule itself says: 'A unified Sangha, mutually rejoicing, without dispute, with one recital, dwells in comfort.'[8] Here the notion of unity is closely connected with the recital of the *pāṭimokkha* on the fortnightly *uposatha*. The sentiment is repeated in the concluding lines to the *pāṭimokkha* recital: 'Therein each and every one should train, with unity, with mutual rejoicing, without disputing.'[9]

11 But we are a little unclear what exactly is meant here: does unity require all monastics to participate, at least potentially, in the same *saṅghakamma*, or only those in one particular monastery? The definition of 'unified' a little below says: ' "Unified" means a Sangha that is of the same communion, staying within the same monastic boundary'.[10] This refers to the Sangha within a particular boundary, rather than the universal Sangha 'of the four directions'.

12 This is clarified further in the passage where the fortnightly recital is laid down:

> 13 Now on that occasion the group of six bhikkhus, according to their assembly, recited the *pāṭimokkha*, each in their own assembly. The Blessed One declared regarding that matter: 'Bhikkhus, you should not, according to your assembly, recite the *pāṭimokkha*, each in your own assembly. Whoever should thus recite, this is an offence of wrong-doing. I allow, bhikkhus, an act of *uposatha* for those who are unified.
>
> 14 And then the bhikkhus thought: 'The Blessed One has laid down "an act of *uposatha* for those who are unified". To what extent is there unification, as far as one monastery, or for the whole earth?' The Blessed One declared regarding that matter: 'I allow, bhikkhus, unification to extend as far as one monastery.'[11]

15 Thus the notion of unity of the Sangha is closely tied to the fortnightly *uposatha* recitation as a ritual affirmation of the Sangha's communal identity. For normal purposes, the Sangha should gather all who live within the same monastic boundary (*sīmā*) to recite the *pāṭimokkha* each fortnight.

---

[8] Pali Vinaya 3.172: *Samaggo hi saṅgho sammodamāno avivadamāno ekuddeso phāsu viharatīti.*

[9] Pali Vinaya 4.207: *Sabbeheva samaggehi sammodamānehi avivadamānehi sikkhitabbanti.*

[10] Pali Vinaya 3.172: *Samaggo nāma saṅgho samānasaṁvāsako samānasīmāyaṁ ṭhito.*

[11] Pali Vinaya 1.105.

16 Defining schism in this way would seem too narrowly legalistic. But the story of Devadatta (and those of the bhikkhus of Kosambi and Campā) depicts a gradual deterioration of harmony, a disintegrative process that persists despite repeated efforts to contain it. The actual performance of the separate *uposathas* is merely the legal act that sets the seal on schism. While this formal act is technically limited to one local Sangha, there is no doubt the repercussions were felt to be relevant for Buddhism generally.

17 And so despite this localization of *saṅghakamma* it seems that on major occasions the Sangha would gather in larger groups to perform acts that were valid throughout the monastic community. Such were the First and Second Councils. These Councils combined aspects of Dhamma and Vinaya, which is hardly surprising since for the Sangha, Vinaya is merely the day-to-day application of Dhamma. The form of the dialogue in the Councils echoes that of the *saṅghakammas*, even though the procedure for a Council is not laid down in the Vinaya as a *saṅghakamma*. The narratives are included in the Vinaya Skandhakas, and both Councils discuss Vinaya issues: for the First Council, the disputed 'lesser and minor rules' and other issues; for the Second Council the 'Ten Points' which prompted the event. In each case, the decisions of the Council are clearly held to be valid throughout the whole of the Buddhist Sangha.

18 Startlingly, this has no precedent or justification in the Vinaya itself. As we have seen, the Vinaya treats acts of *saṅghakamma* as pertaining only to an individual monastery. Only the Buddha laid down rules for the Sangha as a whole. But with the Buddha gone, there is no procedure for universal Sangha decision making. The Elders no doubt did the best they could, and their procedure has met with general agreement in the Sangha since then. But it must be remembered that they acted without explicit justification from the Vinaya.

19 This is not so much of a problem as might appear. Actually, for those of us who live the Vinaya every day, it is obvious that much of it operates as guidelines. There are countless situations that crop up constantly which are not explicitly dealt with in the Vinaya. The Vinaya itself includes principles for how to apply precedents in new situations. Very often, the rules of Vinaya are phrased in a legalistic manner which makes them quite easy to get around in practice, if one is so inclined. And so in Myanmar they

say: 'If you know the Vinaya you can kill a chicken'. It is, perhaps, only in the minds of academics that the Vinaya minutely governs every facet of a monk's life. In real life this is simply impossible. This has nothing to do with the question of whether one takes a rigorist or laxist approach to the rules, emphasizing the letter or the spirit. It is simply to acknowledge the plain fact that the rules only cover a limited amount of contexts, and beyond that we must use our best judgement.

20 As its very name suggests, the Third Council, which we shall see has close connections with the Unity Edicts, stands firmly in the tradition of the Councils. It is presented as an act that is valid throughout the Sangha in exactly the same way as the First and Second Councils. And like them, if one tried to examine the Vinaya itself for justification for the Council, you'd have a hard time. Nevertheless it is accepted within the Vinaya traditions as a valid act.

1.2 Aśoka & unity

21 We should carefully consider exactly what Aśoka had in mind in saying that the 'Sangha has been made unified'. It seems to me quite incredible that Aśoka would take the trouble to create three Edicts across a large area of the Buddhist heartland if he was referring to a mere local dispute. Aśoka had a big mind: he was used to thinking in the broadest pan-Indian terms. Surely when he said the 'Sangha has been made unified' he must have meant the Sangha in a universal sense.

22 Since his language here is derived closely from the well known story of Devadatta, he was implicitly placing this event in that context, seeing the conflict as a serious one threatening the Sangha as a whole, and the corresponding resolution being a similarly magnificent act (with, need one add, altogether pleasant kammic results for the unifier!). While the problematic events at Pāṭaliputta itself may well have involved only one central monastery,[12] the presence of the Unity Edicts in several places makes it certain that Aśoka meant the solution to apply generally, not just in one monastery.

[12] The Aśokārāma or Kukkutārāma.

23 The language Aśoka uses, such as the 'unified Sangha', when used in its technical Vinaya sense, as we have seen, refers to a local Sangha. But this is the only language he has, and he must use this to link the story with the recognized vocabulary. Buddhists at that time, as today, would have understood and used the words in a more informal sense than required by the limited technical definition in the Vinaya.

24 It would, therefore, be going seriously beyond the evidence to assert that the statement that the Sangha has been made unified proves that there had previously been a state of schism.[13] Again, the Vinaya texts usually depict the situations as black & white: either there is a schism or unity. But they are legal texts whose character is to seek clear cut black & white definitions. Reality, unfortunately, always comes in shades of grey. We shall see that the accounts of the Third Council depict a state of unrest, an 'issue' arisen and unresolved that seriously interupts the functioning of the Sangha for many years. This can hardly be depicted as 'unity', yet the state of a formal schism is not reached. It is neither schism nor unity. In such a context the Unity Edicts are in fact exquisitely accurate. They depict the arrival at a state of unity, without asserting that there has been a schism.

25 We should then ask, did Aśoka mean that he had unified the Sangha of one particular school, or the Sangha of all Buddhism? The evidence of the edicts shows unambiguously that Aśoka was entirely non-sectarian and tolerant in his outlook. No sects are mentioned, either by name or by implication. There is a famous list of texts that Aśoka recommends for the bhikkhus and bhikkhunis to study. While there is some doubt about the exact texts that are referred to, they all belong to the early shared strata of non-sectarian Suttas and are not sectarian texts, such as the Abhidhamma. As Bechert says: 'It can clearly be shown by a careful analysis of historical records and inscriptions that the king was not partial towards any section of the Sangha.'[14] Without any serious evidence pointing in another direction, then, we can only conclude that Aśoka meant the entire Sangha was unified.

---

[13] *Contra* SASAKI 1989, 186.

[14] BECHERT, 'Notes on the Formation of Buddhist Sects and the Origins of Mahayana', 26.

26 Aśoka's act signalled a sea change in Sangha/state relations. The Sangha was set up as an international self governing body, and the role of the rulers was to support, not to control. The Vinaya accounts of the First and Second Council mention no royal involvement. It must have taken a major institutional crisis for Aśoka to interfere so dramatically.

27 Could this have arisen due to the sectarian disputes? Could, say, an argument over the exact nature of the arahant's enlightenment lead to such a pass? This hardly seems reasonable. We can only imagine that there was a serious crisis which personally involved Aśoka. When we look at the texts we see that there is in fact one such record: the account of the Pali tradition, especially the Vinaya commentary Samantapāsādikā, and its Chinese version Sudassanavinayavibhāsā.[15] In addition, a short passage from the Mahāsaṅghika Vinaya may give us a clue what actually happened.

1.3 The Third Council

28 The main story tells of the 'Third Council' in Pāṭaliputta, held on account of many corrupt, non-Buddhist heretics[16] seeking gains and honour, many of whom entered the Sangha fraudulently by ordaining themselves, thus making the normal functioning of the Sangha impossible:

[15] The Sudassanavinayavibhāsā is a Sinhalese Vinaya Commentary taken to China and translated by Saṅghabhadra about 489 CE. The title is a reconstruction from the Chinese 善見律毘婆沙 (at T49, № 2034, p. 95, c3 it is referred to as 善見毘婆沙, 'Sudassana-vibhāsā'). This text is little known, despite the fact that there is a good English translation by BAPAT and HIRAKAWA. Bapat and Hirakawa follow the Taishō in treating this as a translation of the Samantapāsādikā, although they note the presence of many differences from the existing Pali text. In fact GURUGE is surely correct to argue that the Sudassanavinayavibhāsā is not a translation of the Samantapāsādikā; while the two have much in common, the differences are too far reaching. The passages I have compared would support the thesis that it was an earlier version of the Sinhala commentary that was used by Buddhaghosa, adapted by him in minor ways to conform to the Mahāvihāravāsin viewpoint. This makes it a uniquely important historical document.

[16] Dīpavaṁsa 6.47: *Tithiyā lābhaṁ disvāna sakkārañca mahārahaṁ/ Saṭṭhimattasahassāni theyya-saṁvāsakā ahū*. Described in more detail at Dīpavaṁsa 6.35 as: *Paṇḍaraṅgā jaṭilā ca ni-gaṇṭhā'celakādikā*, and at Dīpavaṁsa 6.37 as: *Ājīvakā aññaladdhikā nānā*.

> 29 The heretics, whose gain and honour had dwindled to the extent that they failed even to get food and clothing,[17] went forth in the *sāsana* seeking gains and honour, each declaring their own twisted views: 'This is Dhamma, this is Vinaya'. Those who did not gain the going forth, having shaved themselves and putting on the yellow robe, wandered into the monasteries, intruding on the *uposatha*, *pavāraṇā*, and *saṅghakamma*. The bhikkhus did not perform *uposatha* together with them.[18]

30 The details that these monks were misrepresenting Dhamma and Vinaya, and that they intruded on '*uposatha*, *pavāraṇā*, and *saṅghakamma*' leave no doubt that the authors of this passage had the Vinaya precedent of the Saṅghabhedakkhandhaka in mind, just as Aśoka did in his Edicts.[19] The texts are quite consistent in this point: the good monks did not perform *uposatha* with the heretics; in fact, the *uposatha* at the central monastery was interrupted for seven years.[20] This clearly means that there was no schism in the legal sense (*kammabheda*), for this requires that separate *uposathas* be carried out within the same *sīmā*.

31 Accordingly, in the Dīpavaṁsa the first account of the troubles[21] does not mention schism (*bheda*). But, in a seeming contradiction, the second version of the same events[22] mentions *bheda*,[23] saying that 236 years after the Buddha: 'another *bheda* arose for the supreme Theravāda.' This still

---

[17] Cf. Dīpavaṁsa 6.34: *Mahālābho ca sakkāro uppajji buddhasāsane/ Pahīṇalābhasakkārā tithiyā puthuladdhikā.*

[18] Samantapāsādikā 1.53. Also below the bhikkhus say to Aśoka's minister: 'We do not perform *uposatha* with heretics'. ('*Na mayaṁ titthiyehi saddhiṁ uposathaṁ karomāti.*)

[19] Similar concerns are reflected elsewhere, for example in the Sthaviran San-Lun-Xian-Yi, composed by Jia-xiang between 397–419: 'At that time in Magadha there was an *upāsaka* who greatly supported Buddhism. Various heretics for the sake of gains shaved their hair and went forth. Thus there came to be the so-called 'thief-dwelling' bhikkhus, of whom Mahādeva was the chief.' (T45, № 1852, p. 9, a22–24.)

[20] E.g. Dīpavaṁsa 6.36: *Ariyā pesalā lajji na pavisanti uposathaṁ, Sampatte ca vassasate vassaṁ chattiṁsa satāni ca.* Or else Samantapāsādikā 1.53: *Asokārāme sattavassāni uposatho upacchijji.*

[21] Dīpavaṁsa 6.34–42.

[22] Dīpavaṁsa 6.43–58. Due to its haphazard compilation, the Dīpavaṁsa frequently includes more than one version of the same events.

[23] Dīpavaṁsa 6.43. *Nikkhante dutiye vassasate vassāni chattiṁsati, Puna bhedo ajāyitha theravādāna'muttamo.* Other verses use terms related to *bheda*, but there they mean the 'destruction' of the teachings: 6.53–4: *Buddhavacanaṁ bhidiṁsu visuddhakañcanaṁ iva./ Sabbe'pi te bhinnavādā vilomā theravādato ...*

does not suggest that there were separate *uposathas* or anything else that might characterize a formal schism. The Dīpavaṁsa is, of course, mythic verse rather than a legal text, and we need not read the use of *bheda* here as confirming that a schism had in fact occurred. Actually, schism is too strong a word for *bheda*, as *bheda* is used very commonly to mean 'separation, division, analysis', etc., in all sorts of contexts, while schism in English only really corresponds to the more formal idea of *saṅghabheda* as the deliberate division of a monastic community.

32 It is in the Samantapāsādikā that we might expect to find more formal mention of schism. But this does not speak of *bheda* at all. After the problems arose in Pāṭaliputra, Moggaliputtatissa reflects that an 'issue' (*adhikaraṇa*) had arisen in the Sangha.[24] In like manner, the dispute is referred to as an *adhikaraṇa* throughout the following paragraphs. This means that there was a problem demanding resolution by performance of a *saṅghakamma*. If an 'issue' was still pending, there cannot have been a schism at this point, because one does not perform *saṅghakamma* with schismatics. From the Vinaya point of view, there was no schism.

1.4 What were the heretics teaching?

33 The heretical imposters are depicted as propounding many teachings, such as eternalism, partial eternalism, eel-wriggling, and so on, a list familiar to any learned Buddhist as the 62 wrong views refuted in the Brahmajāla Sutta.[25] The mention of the 62 views is conventional, and does not represent the actual views of the heretics.

34 We might wonder why the heretics were described in this way: what are the implications or connotations of these views, as the Buddhists of the time would have seen it? In the Pali canon, the 62 views are all seen as springing from the root heresy of belief in a 'self'. This interpretation is explicitly stated in the Pali Saṁyutta Nikāya:

---

[24] Samantapāsādika 1.53: *Uppannaṁ dāni idaṁ adhikaraṇaṁ, taṁ nacirasseva kakkhaḷaṁ bhavissati. Na kho panetaṁ sakkā imesaṁ majjhe vasantena vūpasametunti.*

[25] DN 1/DA 21/T1 № 21, also in Tibetan and Sanskrit. Cf. Dīpavaṁsa 6.26–33. The Sudassanavinyavibhāsā agrees: T24, № 1462, p. 684, a29–b1.

35 > 'These 62 twisted views taught in the Brahmajāla; these views, householder, exist when identity view exists, when identity view does not exist they do not exist.'[26]

36 But the Sarvāstivādin version of this same Sutta, while similar in other respects, does not mention the 62 views of the Brahmajāla. Instead, the text simply mentions 'views of self, views of a being, views of a soul (*jīva*), views of the auspicious and inauspicious'.[27]

37 This makes us consider whether the emphasis on the 62 views of the Brahmajāla might be a sectarian bias of the Mahāvihāra. Of course the Sutta itself is found in Dharmaguptaka, Sarvāstivādin, and other versions and must be regarded as part of the shared heritage. But there is reason for thinking that the Mahāvihāravāsins treated this particular discourse with special reverence.

38 In their account of the First Council, the Mahāvihāravāsins made the Brahmajāla the first of all Suttas, unlike all other schools we know of except the Dharmaguptaka. Bhikkhu Bodhi suggests that this placement ' ... is not a matter of chance or of haphazard arrangement, but of deliberate design on the part of the Elders who compiled the canon and set it in its current form.'[28] He goes on to reflect on the Dhammic relevance of this position: '... just as our sutta, in terms of its position, stands at the entrance to the total collection of discourses spoken by the Buddha, so does its principle message provide a prolegomenon to the entire Dispensation itself.' Indeed, one might suggest that this Sutta represents the first factor of the eightfold path, right view, while the subsequent Suttas of the Dīgha concentrate on the ethical and meditative components of the path.

39 But while the position of this Sutta fulfils an important Dhammic role, we should not neglect the political dimension of this choice. In asserting that the first priority of the Elders who organized the Dhamma at the First Council was to condemn the 62 kinds of wrong view, the Mahāvihāravāsins established a mythic precedent for the acts of Aśoka and Moggaliputtatissa

---

[26] SN 41.3: *'Yāni cimāni dvāsaṭṭhi diṭṭhigatāni brahmajāle bhaṇitāni; imā kho, gahapati, diṭṭhiyo sakkāyadiṭṭhiyā sati honti, sakkāyadiṭṭhiyā asati na hontī'ti.*

[27] 或說有我或說眾生或說壽命或說世間吉凶 (SA 570 at T2, № 99, p. 151, a12–13).

[28] Bodhi, *The Discourse on the All-embracing Net of Views*, 1.

in cleansing the Sangha from the 62 kinds of wrong view at the Third Council.

40 We begin to suspect that the canonical Mahāvihāravāsin (and also Dharmaguptaka?) account of the First Council has been adjusted to provide a precedent for the Third Council.[29] This suspicion is confirmed when we look at the only other Sutta mentioned in the Mahāvihāravāsin First Council, the Sāmaññaphala Sutta. This concerns the story of Ajātasattu, a powerful king of Magadha, who at the start of his reign had committed a terrible act of violence, but, experiencing dreadful remorse, made a dramatic public confession of his sins, took refuge in the Buddha's Dhamma, and, according to the Mahāvihāravāsin sources, later sponsored the First Council. Aśoka was also a powerful king of Magadha, who at the start of his reign had committed a terrible act of violence, but, experiencing dreadful remorse, made a dramatic public confession of his sins, took refuge in the Buddha's Dhamma, and, according to the Mahāvihāravāsin sources, later sponsored the Third Council. May we be forgiven for seeing another possible connection there?

41 The motivation for emphasizing the Sāmaññaphala would seem to be transparent enough. After Aśoka's coronation, his bloody campaigns, especially at Kalinga, must have been widely loathed by the peaceloving Buddhists. Politics in those days being exactly as cynical as they are today, it would have taken a great deal to convince people that his conversion and remorse were genuine. The story of Ajātasattu could be invoked as a mythic paradigm for Aśoka's sincerity and credibility as a Buddhist sympathizer. This would have been especially crucial in order to justify Aśoka's unprecedented step of actually intervening in the Sangha's internal affairs and deciding who was heretical and who was not.

42 After examining the bad monks and hearing of all their wrong views, Aśoka asks the good monks what the Buddha taught (*kiṁvādī bhante sammāsambuddhoti?*) and they say the Buddha was a *vibhajjavādin* (*vibhajjavādī*

---

[29] On other grounds, I believe the Mahāvihāravāsin account of the recitation of the Vinaya at the First Council was adapted to form a precedent for the Second Council. The symmetry is neat: the Second Council was over a Vinaya dispute, and so corresponds with the Vinaya side of the First Council; the Third Council was over a Dhamma dispute, and so corresponds with the Dhamma side of the First Council.

mahārājāti).[30] This was confirmed by the hero of the story, Moggaliputtatissa, who in the Mahāvihāravāsin accounts is the king's close mentor and adviser, and is regarded by the school as a root teacher. Later we will look more closely at what *vibhajjavāda* means in this context, but for now we will concentrate on those details that can be confirmed in the Edicts.

43 According to the Samantapāsādikā, Aśoka had studied Buddhism under Moggaliputtatissa before the Council and so was able to recognize the false claims of the heretics. He reflected that:

44 > 'These are not bhikkhus, they are recluses from other religions.' Knowing this, he gave them white clothes and expelled them.[31]

45 In this case, the exact words used in the Samantapāsādikā and the Edicts differ, but the meaning is identical.[32] After the bad bhikkhus were expelled, Aśoka declared to Moggaliputtatissa:

46 > 'Now, bhante, the *sāsana* is pure, may the Sangha perform the *uposatha*.' Having given his protection, he entered the city. The Sangha in unity gathered and performed the *uposatha*.[33]

47 As far as the main details go, the Samantapāsādikā and the Edicts are in perfect accord:[34] the Sangha has been made unified; the dividers of the Sangha should be made to wear lay clothes and expelled; this expulsion is associated with the temporal rule of Aśoka rather than being an act of the Sangha; and the event is associated with the *uposatha*.[35]

---

[30] The Dīpavaṁsa does not use the term *vibhajjavādin* here, referring instead to the Theravāda and Sakavāda. *Vibhajjavādin* is found in the commentaries, including the Samantapāsādikā and the Sudassanavinayavibhāsā: 王復更問大德佛法云何答言佛分別說也 (T24, № 1462, p. 684, b4–5).

[31] Samantapāsādikā 1.61. Cp. Dīpavaṁsa 4.52: *Therassa santike rājā uggahevāna sāsanaṁ, Theyyasaṁvāsabhikkhuno nāseti liṅganāsanaṁ.*

[32] The Samantapāsādikā refers to the giving of white lay clothes as: *setakāni vatthāni datvā*; the Edicts have: *odātāni dusāni saṁnaṁdhāpayitu*. Being physically expelled from the monastery is expressed in the Samantapāsādikā as: *uppabbājesi*; in the Edicts as: *anāvāsasi āvāsayiye*. Sudassanavinayavibhāsā has: 王即以白衣服與諸外道驅令罷道 (T24, № 1462, p. 684, b3).

[33] Samantapāsādikā 1.61.

[34] Much academic ink has been spilt on this matter. For alternative points of view see SASAKI, "Buddhist Sects in the Aśoka Period. (1) The Meaning of the Schism Edict".

[35] The only substantial difference is that, for Aśoka, the trouble makers are bhikkhus and bhikkhunis, whereas for the Sri Lankan accounts some are ordained, while others are

48 This version of events also allows us to understand why Aśoka should interfere. It was he who had so lavishly supported the Sangha, inadvertently creating the crisis. While he may or may not have felt any responsibility for the problems, he would have certainly been unhappy about continuing to furnish imposters with their material needs.

49 The whole story is eminently plausible, and is familiar in many countries where Buddhism flourishes today. As soon as the Sangha attracts lavish support from wealthy and generous patrons, there is an influx of bogus monks who are solely interested in ripping off as much money as they can. These are a persistent nuisance and it is difficult or impossible for the Sangha alone to deal with them. They flourish unchecked unless the Government has the will power to forcibly remove their robes and prevent them from harassing and deceiving Buddhist donors.

50 The fact that Aśoka expelled the fake monks and made them revert to lay clothes is a crucial detail. The opponents at this Council were not Buddhist monks who differed in interpretation of certain doctrinal points, they were non-Buddhists, not deserving of being monks at all. Though the Mahāvihāravāsins claimed to be the only non-schismatic sect, even they did not go so far as to assert that members of other schools must be disrobed. Even if we were to accept the Mahāvihāravāsin position that all other schools were schismatic in the literal sense defined in Vinaya, this would simply mean the communities could not share the same communal *uposatha* recitation. It does not mean the opponents are not monks: in fact, only bhikkhus can cause a schism, so if the opponents at the Third Council were really laypeople, there is no way they could cause a schism. The only recourse would be to recognize their fraudulent status and expel them. So the story of the Third Council is not, from the Aśokan or the Mahāvihāravāsin point of view, the story of a schism. In fact, the mainstream Mahāvihāravāsin Vinaya commentary, in both the Pali and Chinese versions, does not mention schism at all.

51 It seems to me that the implications of these 'schism' edicts have been brushed aside by scholars due to their predisposition, based primarily on

---

theyyasaṁvāsika, fraudulent pretenders who just put the robes on themselves and are not really ordained. But this is a minor point, since these may also be referred to as *theyyasaṁvāsika* bhikkhus, and the edicts are doubtless not concerned with such legal niceties.

the textual accounts of the Dīpavaṁsa and Vasumitra, to see the schisms as pre-Aśoka. Thus Cousins says: 'If there were different Buddhist fraternities at this time, and at least the difference between the Vinaya traditions of Mahāsaṅghika and Theravāda/Theriya is likely to be earlier than this date, then the king would have taken no account of that.'[36] Lamotte, with equally little attempt at justification, says: 'The king's intentions were to force dissidents to return to lay status ... However, his orders were not followed.'[37] Warder says: 'It is not known what Aśoka proposed to do about the fact that the Buddhists were already split into at least five schools.'[38] None of these interpretations attempt to grapple seriously with the undeniable fact that none of Aśoka's words give any hint that different Buddhist sects existed in his time.

1.5 Aśoka in the Mahāsaṅghika Vinaya?

52 Sasaki points out that a unique passage in the Mahāsaṅghika Vinaya may be referring to Aśoka's involvement in the returning of schismatic monks to lay status. The relevant passage appears in the Mahāsaṅghika Vinaya Skandhaka, according to Sasaki, at just the point where it breaks away from the pattern of the other Sthavira Skandhakas. He therefore suggests that this episode, based on real events in Aśoka's time, was a crucial influence in stimulating the reshaping of the Mahāsaṅghika Vinaya. Here is his translation of the relevant passage:

> 53 If the monks have noticed that a particular monk is going to do *saṅghabheda* they must say to him: 'Venerable, do not do *saṅghabheda*. *Saṅghabheda* is a serious sin. You will fall into an evil state of being or go to hell. I will give you clothes and an alms-bowl. I will instruct you in the Sūtras and read Sūtras for you. If you have some question, I will teach you.'
>
> 54 If he still does not stop it, they must say to a powerful *upāsaka*: 'Mr. So-and-so is going to do *saṅghabheda*. Go and dissuade him from doing it.' The *upāsaka* must say to [the monk]: 'Venerable, do not do *saṅghabheda*. *Saṅghabheda* is a serious sin. You will fall into an

[36] COUSINS, 'On the Vibhajjavādins', 138.
[37] LAMOTTE, *History of Indian Buddhism*, 238.
[38] WARDER, 262.

evil state of being or go to hell. I will give you clothes, an alms-bowl, and medicine for curing illness. If you feel dullness in the life of a monk return to secular life. I will find a wife for you and give you the necessities of life.'

55 If he still does not stop it, the monks must dismiss him by removing the *śalāka* (voting stick) that indicates his membership [in the Sangha]. After dismissing him, the Sangha must proclaim as follows: 'Everybody! There is a man who is plotting *saṅghabheda*. If he approaches you, watch out!'

56 If, despite these precautions, he has done *saṅghabheda* it is called '*saṅghabheda*' ...[39]

57 Sasaki believes that the unique phrase 'powerful *upāsaka*' refers to none other than Aśoka himself. His acts in persuading the bad monks to return to lay life here come across more like a social security safety net than a shameful expulsion. This would make sense if we see the bad monks as freeloaders and opportunists, rather than heretics trying to destroy Buddhism, or genuine Buddhists developing a new doctrine or practice. If they had simply joined the Sangha to scrounge a living, offering to support their needs after disrobal may have been a means of non-confrontational problem solving.

58 Like our other sources, this text falls well short of establishing that a schism occurred during Aśoka's reign. First we must remember that the connection with Aśoka is, of course, speculative, and the passage might as well refer to something quite different. It only discusses theoretical events, and does not assert that a schism occurred. And the stage of calling upon a 'powerful *upāsaka*' is only the second of three preliminary stages before a schism can occur. Even if, as I think quite possible, the passage does in fact refer to the same actual events as the Unity Edicts and the Third Council, there is no need to suppose that all three stages were completed. In fact, our only source on the event as a whole, the Third Council narratives, asserts that the intervention of the 'powerful *upāsaka*' was effective and schism was averted.

59 It is also crucial to notice that if this did refer to an actual schism, it must have been the root schism between the Mahāsaṅghikas and the

---

[39] SASAKI, "Buddhist Sects in the Aśoka Period. (1) The Meaning of the Schism Edict", 193–194. Translation slightly modified. Original text at T22, № 1425, p. 441, a11–23.

Sthaviras. But this is highly problematic. Our source is the Mahāsaṅghika Vinaya, but the Mahāsaṅghika Śāriputraparipṛcchā puts the root schism much later, which would entail a gross inconsistency on this issue within the Mahāsaṅghikas. Even worse, our three sources—from the Sthavira, Mahāsaṅghika, and Aśokan points of view—all take the same side, against the schismatic monks who are returned to lay life. It is impossible that these could represent opposing sides in the debate. The simplest interpretation of our sources is to agree that there was no schism at this time.

Chapter 2

THE SAINTS OF VEDISA

OUR NEXT EVIDENCE for the date of the schisms derives from the relic caskets of the ancient Hemavata teachers, which has recently been clarified by Michael Willis.

2 The reliquaries have been dated to around the end of the second century BCE, that is, a little over a century after Aśoka. These inscriptions are our oldest epigraphic evidence for personal names, locations, and dates of monks. Willis shows that five monks mentioned on the caskets may be identified with five monks who, as recorded in the Samantapāsādikā and other Pali sources, were sent to the Himalayan region as part of the Aśokan missionary effort. Additional names are the students and followers of the original missionaries. Thus the Pali sources find important verification in our two oldest sources of epigraphical information: the Aśokan Edicts confirm the Third Council, and the Vedisa inscriptions confirm the account of the missions.[1]

3 The reliquaries describe these monks as the 'teachers of all the Himalaya'. Hence we must also see this group as the fraternity that later sources would

[1] One of the missions is supposed to have gone to Suvaṇṇabhūmi, usually identified with Thaton in Burma or Nakorn Pathom in Thailand. But Buddhism is usually said to have arrived there much later. Hence Lamotte asserts that the missions account could not have been compiled before the 5th century (LAMOTTE, *History of Indian Buddhism*, 298). But the identification of Suvaṇṇabhūmi with this region is uncertain. Thus the later arrival of Buddhism in Southeast Asia, even if true, cannot be used as proof that the mention of an Aśokan mission to Suvaṇṇabhūmi is unhistorical. See discussion at http://web.ukonline.co.uk/buddhism/tawsein8.htm.

Table 2.1: Hemavata Teachers

Pali texts	Reliquaries at Sonārī stupa 2	Reliquaries at Sāñchī stupa 2	Reliquaries at Andher
Majjhima	Majhima Koṣinīputa	Majhima/ Koṣinīputa	
Kassapagotta	Kotīputa Kāsapagota	Kāsapagota	
Ālavakadeva	Ālābagira	Āpa(=Āla?)gira	
Sahadeva	Kosikiputa	Kosīkiputa	
Dundubhissara	Gotiputa Dudubhisaradāyāda	Gotiputa	
		Hāritīputa	Hāritiputa
		Mogaliputa	Mogaliputa, pupil of Gotiputa
		Vāchiya Suvijayita, pupil of Goti[puta]	Vāchiputa, pupil of Gotiputa
		Mahavanāya	

describe as the 'Himalayan School' (Haimavata Nikāya). I would question, however, to what extent the epigraphic evidence allows us to conclude that a 'school' existed at that time.

4 Clearly, there are many elements that are essential for the creation of a 'school'. We see a tightly bound group, all of whom would have known each other, with common teachers. We see the arising of a cult of worshipping local saints, as well as the Buddha and the great disciples who were honoured by all Buddhists. We see a well developed and lavishly supported institutional centre.

5 But there are also many things we do not see. We don't, so far as I am aware, see the use of the term *nikāya* or other terms denoting a school. We have no evidence of a separate textual lineage, or independently developed doctrines. We have no evidence that this group carried out separate *saṅghakamma*.

6 I would suggest that, simply reading the evidence in the most literal way as we did with the Aśokan edicts, the Vedisa inscriptions show that

a centre was developed around a monastic group that at a later date was known as the Haimavata school. We do not know whether they regarded themselves as a distinct 'school' at this stage. Rather than seeing the Vedisa finds as evidence that schools already existed at this date, we would be better to consider this evidence for what it can teach us regarding how schools emerge.

7 While identification of the Himalayan missionaries is fairly certain, the rest of the names present us with some intriguing questions.

2.1 Gotiputa

8 Gotiputa was obviously an important monk, and was probably instrumental in establishing the Hemavata presence at Vedisa. Willis puts his date at roughly mid-second century BCE.[2] However, this conclusion rests on several quite flexible assumptions, and really Gotiputa and his disciples may have lived any time between the mission period and the erection of the stupas.[3]

9 Gotiputa is said to be the 'heir' (*dāyāda*) of one of the original five missionaries, Dundubhissara. The appellation *dāyāda* is not a regular Vinaya term indicating a direct student-teacher relationship, so Willis takes it to indicate that Gotiputa lived some time after the original mission. However, the meaning of *dāyāda* would seem to rather imply an intimate living relationship, rather than a distant inheritor of a lineage. In the spiritual sense (*dhammadāyāda* or *sāsanadāyāda*) it means one who is truly worthy of the living religion. In a more mundane sense, an inheritor is one who is the most worthy to receive the material possessions of one who has died. Thus for laypeople in the patriarchal society of the time, the son is the inheritor rather than the sister.[4] When a monk dies, his belongings return to the Sangha. However, since a nurse is of great benefit, the Sangha is encouraged to give the dead monk's requisites to the attendant monk who was looking after the deceased.[5] In the Mahāsaṅghika Vinaya the monk

---

[2] WILLIS, 228.

[3] See http://sectsandsectarianism.santipada.org/namesanddatesatvedisa.

[4] Pali Vinaya 3.66.

[5] Pali Vinaya 1.303.

who inherits the requisites is not merely a direct student (*saddhivihārika* or *antevāsin*), but must be also trustworthy and agreed upon by the Sangha.[6] The word *dāyāda* is not used in this context in the Pali Vinaya. Nevertheless, I think these examples show that a *dāyāda* is more likely to be a special, closely 'anointed' heir, rather than a distant descendant from the same lineage. In this sense it may be more intimate than 'student' (*antevāsi*), for a teacher may have any number of students, and while the teacher and student are ideally supposed to regard each other like father and son, in reality they may not have any specially close relationship. This would also suit our context, for it would exalt Gotiputa's status more if he was seen as being the one truly worthy of carrying on Dundubhissara's mission after his death. If the relationship of *dāyāda* is something like we have proposed, then it would seem likely that Gotiputa was a younger contemporary of the original Hemavata teachers.

10 We next feel obliged to ask, who then was this Gotiputa? He was clearly an important teacher. But he is mysteriously unknown—or is he? The Vinaya commentary account of the Third Council tells the following story. I translate from the Chinese, which in this case is similar to the Pali:

> 11 At that time, king Aśoka had ascended the throne for 9 years. There was one bhikkhu, called Kotaputtatissa,[7] who became severely ill. Walking for alms for medicine, he received but a pinch of ghee. The illness grew until his life force was ending. He approached the bhikkhus and said: 'In the three realms, be watchful, not lazy!' Having said this, he flew into the air. Seated in space, he entered the fire element, burned up his body and entered Nibbana. At that time king Aśoka heard people speak of this, and then made offerings. The king reflected and said: 'Even in my realm the bhikkhus who need medication cannot get it! ... '[8]

12 Here we have a teacher whose name would seem uncannily similar to the Haimavata teacher of the inscriptions. Pali variants of his name include

---

6 T 1425, 479b23–c23. Translation at WALSER, 143–145.

7 拘多子。名帝須 (T24, № 1462, p. 682, a15–16). This is, of course, only an approximation of the Indic form.

8 爾時阿育王登位九年。有比丘拘多子。名帝須。病困劇。持鉢乞藥得酥一撮。其病增長命將欲斷。向諸比丘言。三界中愼勿懈怠。語已飛騰虛空。於虛空中而坐即化作火自焚燒身。入於涅盤。是時阿育王。聞人宣傳爲作供養。王念言。我國中比丘。求藥而不能得 (T24, № 1462, p. 682, a15–21).

Kontiputta, Kuntaputta, and Kontaputta.[9] The relic inscriptions include the forms Kotīputa and Gotiputa.[10] It seems that these are two different monks, for these two forms appear on two reliquaries discovered as part of the same collection of five.

13 However, might there not be some kind of family connection?[11] The language of the inscriptions regularly contracts what are formed as consonant clusters in Pali or Sanskrit; thus, for example, the Pali Dundubhissara becomes Dudubhisara in the inscriptions. We also note several cases on the caskets where the spelling oscillates between *i* and *ī*. Jayawickrama suggests the identification of Goti- and Kotī-, pointing out the change of g→k in Northwestern Prākrits[12] (although we are not in the North-west!). Without concluding one way or the other, we raise the possibility that these are variant forms of the same name. But if there is a family connection, exactly what kind of family are we talking about?

14 The Mahāvaṁsa elaborates the story. Kontiputtatissa is the son of a *kinnarī* (wood-nymph) called Kuntī, who was seduced by a man from Pāṭaliputta and 'it seems' (*kira*) gave birth to two sons, Tissa and Sumitta. They both went forth under the elder Mahāvaruṇa.[13] (Evidently having a wood-nymph as mother does not disqualify one from being considered a 'human being' for ordination purposes.) Kontiputtatissa was bitten by an insect, but although he told his brother that a handful of ghee was needed as cure, he would not go in search of it after his meal. This version agrees with the others in the manner of Kontiputtatissa's death. All versions also concur that Aśoka's remorse in hearing of the story caused him to dramatically increase his already generous support of the Sangha, motivating corrupt elements to enter the Sangha and precipitating the crisis that led to the Third Council. We notice that Kontiputtatissa's brother Sumitta also died within the year. This story of the wood-nymph and her two ill-fated

---

[9] Jayawickrama, 1986, 173.

[10] Willis, 223.

[11] As suggested by Jayawickrama, 105 note 53.1.

[12] Jayawickrama, 108.

[13] Mahāvaruṇa was also the preceptor of Nigrodha, the novice who inspired Aśoka to become a Buddhist.

sons adds an intriguing dimension to our story.[14] But for now it is enough to notice that the 'Kuntī' clan appear to have been no ordinary family.

2.2 Mogaliputa

15 Now, Gotiputa had a number of students, prominently a certain 'Mogaliputa' and 'Vāchiputa'. One lineage of scholars, starting with Cunningham and Geiger, makes the obvious connection between this Mogaliputa and the Moggaliputtatissa of the Pali chronicles. Another lineage, including Lamotte and Willis, dismiss this identification out of hand. Both the reasons for making the equation and those for dismissing it are fairly simple. Here we have a certain monk, clearly associated with the same general period and the missionary activities of the same five monks, and sharing the same name. The problem is that in the Pali accounts, Moggaliputtatissa lived at the time of Aśoka, whereas the student of Gotiputa, if Willis' dating is correct, must have lived over a century later. But when we recognize that such datings are based on assumptions that are flexible if not entirely arbitrary, we cannot be so certain about fixing Gotiputa's date on the archaeological evidence.

16 A further problem with identifying Moggaliputtatissa of the Pali tradition with Mogaliputa of the relic caskets is that Moggaliputtatissa was supposed to be the leader of the Hemavata teachers. If we equate the two, however, we end up with Moggaliputtatissa being the student of the heir of the Hemavata teachers.

17 But the placement of Moggaliputtatissa as leader of the missions is to some extent an expression of Mahāvihāravāsin bias. Clearly, there were many Elder monks involved. The missions were, in all likelihood, organized by a loosely associated group of Elders who took advantage of the favourable conditions of Aśoka's reign to spread the Dhamma. And the organizer need not be the most senior: the leading monk was not the most senior at either the First or the Second Councils. The missions involved at least three generations of monks: Moggaliputtatissa, Majjhantika, and Mahādeva presided over Mahinda's ordination, and Mahinda in turn took a number of disciples, including a novice, with him to Sri Lanka. We are

[14] See *White Bones Red Rot Black Snakes*, Ch. 7.

perfectly in accord with the texts, therefore, to assume that the Hemavata teachers were roughly equal in rank to Moggaliputtatissa.

18 One unspoken assumption of Willis' reasoning is that the information on the relic caskets, since it is concrete, dateable, and placable, is likely to be accurate. Of course, this is a reasonable assumption—but reasonable assumptions are not always true. From the earliest times, we can assume that the communities were jockeying for position, aiming to have their own lineage regarded as supreme. Those who were writing inscriptions on reliquaries were no more or less concerned with creating an accurate historical record than were those who compiled edifying chronicles.

19 We know that the positions of prominent elders in the lineage lists are not consistent. A well known example is that of Majjhantika. In the Pali, he is an Aśokan missionary; but in the northern sources he is usually depicted as a direct disciple of Ānanda. This is because he was a contemporary of Śāṇavāsin and Upagupta, who represent the Mathura lineage, and the Kaśmīr lineage had to be incorporated in the well established Mathuran lineage, which allowed the Kaśmīr patriarch to be depicted as the senior. Similarly, the Sinhala Vinaya Commentary depicts Siggava and Caṇḍavajji as the teachers of Moggaliputtatissa. But later Chinese sources say Caṇḍavajji was Moggaliputtatissa's student.[15]

20 We can therefore regard the difference in perspective between the Pali texts and the inscriptions as being, not an irreconcilable gulf, but an entirely normal presentation according to the bias of each school. The Mahāvihāravāsins regarded Moggaliputtatissa as the definer of their doctrinal position, and hence wished to place him at the centre of the missionary activity. The Hemavatas, quite understandably, wished to emphasize the importance of their own lineage, so placed their own teachers at a higher rank than Moggaliputtatissa.

21 There is one other minor point that might be felt to strengthen the association between the two 'Moggaliputtas'. In the Dīpavaṁsa, Aśoka, disappointed by the heretics, is said to wonder when he might have the chance to meet a *sappurisa*, who of course turns out to be Moggaliputtatissa. This is a well known canonical term denoting an *ariya*, one who has reached

---

[15] 目揵連子帝須欲涅槃付弟子旃陀跋闍 (T49, № 2034, p. 95, b26–27). Also at T55, № 2154, p. 535, c19.

the noble path. The relic casket refers to the monks as *sappurisa*, including *sapurisa mogaliputa*. This shows at least that the term was in common use in these contexts, and might well have been used of the same person.

2.3 Vāchiputa

22 In another striking coincidence, Vāchiputa, student (*antevāsī*) of Gotiputa, has the same name as the founder of the Puggalavāda ('Personalist') schools.[16] The chief doctrine of this group of schools is that there exists a 'person' (*puggala*), which is not a 'self' (*attā*), and is indescribable, being neither identical with or different from the five aggregates. This group of schools is not clearly differentiated, and it may be that the same school is known after its teacher as 'Vātsīputrīya', and after its chief doctrine as 'Puggalavāda' (just as the Mahāvihāravāsins are known after their doctrine as *vibhajjavādins*, and after their being followers of the 'Elders' as Theriyas).

23 While the Puggalavādins and their founder Vātsīputra are not explicitly mentioned in the Third Council narrative, their chief doctrine is extensively discussed in the Kathāvatthu attributed to Moggaliputtatissa, so there is clearly a strong connection, even if a negative one. The Puggalavādin's own tradition, preserved by Bhavya, puts the foundation of their school by Vātsīputra in 200 AN; he would therefore be roughly contemporary with Moggaliputtatissa. Cousins suggests that if the Vāchiputa of the inscriptions is indeed the founder of the Puggalavādins, then it must be he who is debating with Moggaliputtatissa in the Kathāvatthu.

24 It might seem strange to find these two monks remembered as students of the same teacher, for Moggaliputtatissa is an avowed anti-personalist, whose main doctrinal legacy according to both the Mahāvihāravāsins and Sarvāstivādins is his attack on the 'person' doctrine. But a little reflection would suggest that this is in fact most likely, for it is with our closest family and friends that we have our deepest disagreements. If the schools had just drifted apart with no clear doctrinal disagreements, like the Dharmaguptaka and Mahāvihāravāsins, there would be no cause for disputes. But living close together, sharing students and lay supporters, differences may well harden, leaving a bitterness that lasts through the ages.

[16] Cf. COUSINS, 'Person and Self', 86.

25 Xuan-zang records the tradition that the debate on the 'person' emerged from the conflict between the two arahants Devaśarman, author of the Vijñānakāya, and Gopa near Viśoka.[17] Cousins notes the similarity of the names 'Gopa' and 'Gotiputa' in this connection, both evidently derived from the √*gup*, and wonders whether the name of the teacher has replaced that of the pupil.[18]

26 Willis and Lamotte dismissed the identification of Mogaliputa with Moggaliputtatissa, with Willis arguing that it is simpler to accept that there were two Elders of the same name. But if not one, but three names—Moggaliputta, Vāchiputta, Kontiputta—associated with the Third Council narrative appear in the inscriptions, the balance of probabilities shift, and we may want to reassess our conclusions.

27 We can only speculate about the true identities of these monks. In life they were complex and paradoxical humans, but they appear to us as mere names, an an echo of an idea, and fragments of burnt bone. So desperate is our groping for knowledge that we are delighted to find just this much. How much more should we appreciate the confidence with which the Vedisa inscriptions confirm the missions account. It is quite remarkable that the only two pieces of substantial epigraphical evidence from this period both agree strongly with the account preserved by the Sinhalese Vinaya commentarial tradition.

28 While we will not take the time to discuss this in detail here, there are further evidences that support the missions account, although they are not as clear-cut. Aśoka claims to have sent out 'messengers' (or 'missionaries', *dūta*) to accomplish his 'Dhamma-victory'. Wynne shows that these need to be distinguished from Aśoka's 'Dhamma-ministers', who are involved in secular social work within the empire.[19] The messengers went outside the empire and were engaged in religious or ethical teaching. Wynne concludes that these were likely to have been the Buddhist monks of the missions. Finally, we should notice that the archaeological record in Sri Lanka conforms with the chronology, events, and places described in

---

[17] T51, № 2087, p. 898, c15–17. For Xuan-zang it is apparently not impossible for two arahants to disagree over such a fundamental doctrine, suggesting that a difference in conceptual expression of Dhamma does not imply difference in realization.

[18] Cousins, 'Person and Self', 86.

[19] Wynne, 12–21.

the missions account.[20] Writing has been discovered in Sri Lanka dating from the 5th century BCE, earlier than anywhere else in India, and even the pre-Buddhist legends of Sri Lankan colonization in this period seem to have some foundation. While there is no definitive reference to the missions yet found, the stones are telling the same kind of story as the missions accounts. In the next chapters we shall see that this evidence just as strongly disagrees with most of the other textual evidence.

[20] ALLCHIN, 156–183.

Chapter 3

THE DĪPAVAṀSA

HAVING CONSIDERED THE EPIGRAPHICAL EVIDENCE, I would like to now turn to the later textual accounts. We have seen that important parts of the Pali tradition have been confirmed by the epigraphical findings. With the possible exception of the passage from the Mahāsaṅghika Vinaya discussed earlier, the northern traditions are entirely lacking in archaeological support for this period. But this does not mean that we should accept the Mahāvihāravāsin tradition *in toto*. I have already indicated my severe reservations about the Dīpavaṁsa's account of the formation of the schools, and it is this that we now consider. The principle question is whether we can accept the Dīpavaṁsa's identification of the Mahāsaṅghikas with the laxist Vajjiputtakas of the Second Council.

2 Recent scholarship applauds the death of the Dīpavaṁsa's theory. But certain scholars, having attended the funeral in the sunny afternoon, return in the deep of night with a shovel. They dig the earth, still soft, and disturb the corpse from the sleep of eternity which it well deserved. With diverse wierdings and incantations they infuse it with a vitality that is unnatural, and set it to its awful task: to destroy the younglings that they should not grow to the fullness of new life. My mission is to cut off the Dīpavaṁsa schism theory like a palm-tree stump, so that it is no longer subject to future arising; then chop the wood into chips, burn the chips, and disperse the ashes in the wind.

3 Obviously I do not wish to criticize the Dīpavaṁsa in general. Nor do I wish to criticize everything about the Dīpavaṁsa's account of the sects: the sequence of arising of sects and their mutual interrelationships is, generally speaking, no less plausible than any other; and the fact that the text ascribes the root schism to a dispute on textual redaction has an element of plausibility.

4 Specifically, I wish to refute the Dīpavaṁsa's assertion that the Mahāsaṅghikas originated from a reformed group of Vajjiputtakas who held a separate 'Great Council' after the Second Council. This is supported by no other source and contradicts the central message of the Second Council as recorded in all the Vinayas: the dispute was successfully resolved.

5 A close reading of the Dīpavaṁsa shows that the passage on the schisms is an interpolation into a separate passage dealing with the Second and Third Councils. Dīpavaṁsa 4.68 clearly expresses the conclusion of the Second Council: *Aṭṭhamāsehi niṭṭhāsi dutiyo saṅgaho ayan'ti* ('In eight months the Second Council was completed.') Here the word *niṭṭhāsi* conveys completion, telling us the story was supposed to end here. This terminological hint is backed up with a syntactic feature: the line ends with the particle *-ti*, which indicates the end of a section. Thus the Second Council as narrated in the Dīpavaṁsa (or its source) originally concluded with the successful resolution of the Council, in accord with all the Vinaya accounts.

6 These textual details may be ambiguous, but there's more. Following this closure of the Second Council, the Dīpavaṁsa goes on to give the account of the emergence of the Mahāsaṅghika and the subsequent schisms leading to the formation of all eighteen schools. Obviously this must have been a process that took many years. But following all this Dīpavaṁsa 5.1 links back to the Second Council:

7 In the future, in a hundred years and eighteen,
Will arise that bhikkhu, a proper ascetic.[1]

8 The 'proper ascetic' is Moggaliputtatissa, and in the Dīpavaṁsa's chronology the date of '118 years in the future' is the period between the Second and Third Councils. In other words this phrase, though supposedly set after the entire schismatic process, is spoken from the point of view im-

[1] *Anāgate vassasate vassāna'ṭṭhārasāni ca/Uppajjissati so bhikkhu samaṇo paṭirūpako.* Here *paṭirūpaka* obviously does not mean 'counterfeit'.

mediately following the Second Council. The entire story of the schisms has been interpolated here, leaving the '118 years in the future' hanging without context. We could ask for no clearer indication that the entire account of the schisms and the formation of the Mahāsaṅghika is foreign to the account of the Councils.

9 Noting that the schisms account is entirely absent from the Vinaya commentaries, Cousins concludes that: 'This strongly suggests that no account of the "eighteen schools" was preserved in the commentarial tradition of the Mahāvihāra.'[2] He further remarks: 'Erich Frauwallner has presented evidence that the account of the formation of the eighteen schools in the Dīpavaṁsa does not derive from the old commentarial tradition of the Mahāvihāra and may in fact be from an Abhayagiri source ...'.[3] In any case, the passage is closely related to Vasumitra, Bhavya I, and the Śāriputraparipṛcchā, and hence clearly derives from a 'northern' source. It is ironic that the text that so strongly condemns all other schools itself contains a corrupt interpolation. The Mahāvihāra would have been better off sticking to their own more reliable commentarial traditions.

10 In accepting this northern source and attempting to reconcile it with their own quite different history, the Mahāvihāra inevitably ended up with an incoherent account. The authors of the Second Council passages, both in the Vinayas and the Dīpavaṁsa, intended this to be read as the story of a significant trauma in Buddhist history, one which nevertheless was surmounted in harmony due to the diligent application of the principles of the Vinaya. Crucially, the Mahāsaṅghikas maintain exactly the same tradition in their own Vinaya. They have the same rules prohibiting the use of money as found in all other schools. Accordingly, they condemn the Vajjiputtakas, refute them in the Second Council, and conclude their Council passage by saying: 'Thus all Elders should train together in harmony'.[4]

11 In attempting to fuse the account of the Council and the schisms, the Dīpavaṁsa obscures the plain fact that the problematic issues discussed in relation to the Vajjiputtakas in the Second Council have precisely nothing in common with the issues concerning the Mahāsaṅghikas of the 'Great

[2] COUSINS, 'The "Five Points" and the Origins of the Buddhist Schools', 56.

[3] COUSINS, 'On the Vibhajjavādins', 153.

[4] 如是諸長老應當隨順學 (T22, № 1425, p. 493, c10).

Council'. The Second Council accuses the Vajjiputtakas of the 10 points of laxity in Vinaya. But the story of the Mahāsaṅghika schism in the Dīpavaṁsa says nothing about Vinaya. There the crucial issue was a reshaping of the Buddhist scriptures. We must be clear about this: despite statements to the contrary by some modern scholars,[5] the Dīpavaṁsa does *not* ascribe the schism to the 10 points. Rather, it relates the Second Council narrative including the 10 points, then proceeds to describe how the defeated Vajjiputtakas reformed as the Mahāsaṅghikas[6] and revised the texts. The connection between the Mahāsaṅghikas and the 10 points is a narrative sleight-of-hand: it is the work of Māra. We are conditioned by the former passage to read the 10 points into the later passage; this is the narrative intent of the Dīpavaṁsa. But once we realize the two accounts have completely different origins, any connection between the Mahāsaṅghikas and the 10 points vanishes. Like a sky-flower, it was a mind-made illusion.

12 The very idea that the Mahāsaṅghikas could have rejected the texts directly contradicts a crucial assumption of the whole Second Council story, that is, that the Sangha reached agreement regarding the 10 Vinaya issues by referring to their shared disciplinary code. All freely participated in the Council, and all agreed to solve the problem by appointing a committee of eight, whose verdict, since it was carefully justified point by point against the universally accepted Vinaya rules, was accepted by all. If the Vajjiputtakas were interested in textual revision, they would surely have contested the textual references put forward by the committee.

13 A further difficulty with the Dīpavaṁsa's position is that it assumes that the Vajjiputtakas could blithely ignore the Second Council and make their own schism without any response from the rest of the Sangha. This is absurd, since the events that triggered the Second Council itself were of less importance than a major schism, yet monks gathered from all over Buddhist India. Every other account we have of the root schism tells of a gathering of monks who disputed at length, and split only after failing to find a resolution.

14 This objection is particularly telling when considered in light of the Samantapāsādikā's account of what happened after the Second Council.

---

5 E.g. NATTIER and PREBISH, 200.

6 The Dīpavaṁsa usually uses the term Mahāsaṅgītikas.

The Elders (unnamed) considered whether another disaster would afflict the *sāsana*, and saw that in 118 years in the time of Aśoka, many monks would enter the Sangha seeking gains and fame. They considered how to avert this, and saw that the only being capable was a Brahma named Tissa. They went to the Brahma world, and begged Tissa to descend to save Buddhism.[7] He agreed—how could it be otherwise?—whereupon the Elders returned to the human realm and organized a couple of young arahants, Siggava and Caṇḍavajji, to teach the Brahma when he was reborn as Moggaliputtatissa. This is a wonderfully dramatic scene setter for the Third Council. But if we accept the Dīpavaṁsa's account, then while the Elders were making such elaborate preparations for saving Buddhism in the future, under their very noses the Vajjiputtakas were destroying the unity of the Sangha forever. (Perhaps they were away in the Brahma world while this was going on.)

After describing the root schism, the Dīpavaṁsa tells us that the various schools split off from each other one by one. It doesn't mention any reasons for why this multitude of schisms occurred, nor why they should happen so quickly. Nevertheless, the whole process was over and done with and the 'eighteen' schools were all formed before the time of Aśoka. The Second Council was in 100 AN, and since the Dīpavaṁsa is a 'long chronology' text, this allows 118 years for the schools to form.[8] This is short enough, but if we follow the median chronology we have only 40 years or so. The process of forming a sect in a religion like Buddhism is not easy. It requires a charismatic leader, one who can articulate a convincing independent interpretation of the teachings, inspiring both monastics and lay followers. It requires a certain degree of geographical separation for building an independent lay support. It requires building an institutional basis, i.e. at least one monastery, with shrines, meeting hall, residential quarters, and so on. According to the Dīpavaṁsa, all of this happened within one or two generations, leaving not a single physical trace. This contrasts with other accounts like the Śāriputraparipṛcchā, which give the process several centuries to unfold.

---

7 A mythic mirror-image of the 'Entreaty by Brahma' that motivated the Buddha to teach.

8 See Appendix A.

16 Perhaps even more implausibly, this account implies that in the following centuries there were hardly any new sects. It is true, the commentaries do mention a few schools that arose subsequently, but we are expected to believe that 'eighteen' schools arose almost immediately, and in a thousand years after that only a small number of new schools gradually came to be.

17 A crucial consequence of the Dīpavaṁsa's view would be that the Aśokan missions were 'Theravādins' in the narrow sense, meaning the same school as the Mahāvihāravāsins, rather than the Sthaviras or Vibhajjavādins in general. Thus the Theravādins alone were responsible for converting virtually the whole of India to Buddhism, a situation which blatantly contradicts all the available epigraphic and textual evidence.

18 It may seem ungenerous to impute to the Theravādins the idea that they themselves spread Buddhism over all of India, an idea of breathtaking conceit. But the main epigraphic evidence for the school from the mainland confirms exactly that. Two inscriptions from the Sinhalese monastery in Nāgārjunikoṇḍa, dated to around 250 CE, refer to the teachers of the 'Theriyas, Vibhajjavādas, Mahāvihāravāsins', who have brought faith to various lands: Kaśmīr, Gandhāra, Yava[na] (= Yonaloka of the mission accounts = Greek Bactria), Vanavāsi, Cīna-Cilāta, Tosali, Avaraṁta, Vaṅga, Da[mila], [Pa]lura, and Tambapaṇṇidīpa.[9] This evidence predates the Dīpavaṁsa and the mission accounts, but the similarity of the phrasing, as demonstrated by Cousins, shows that they must derive from a common source, presumably the old Sinhalese tradition.

19 The Mahāvihāravāsins wanted to portray themselves at the centre of Buddhism. The unique creative genius of the Dīpavaṁsa is to enshrine this world view within the fundamental myth of Buddhism. Right from the outset it declares that the Buddha, during the seven days after his awakening, surveyed the world, saw Sri Lanka, and predicted the advent of his Dhamma there after the Third Council.[10] The unified Sangha is referred to as the 'Theravāda' from the time of the First Council on.[11] There is no doubt, given the opening passages, that by this the Dīpavaṁsa,

---

[9] EI, XX, 1929, 22. See LAMOTTE, *History of Indian Buddhism*, 299; COUSINS, 'On the Vibhajjavādins', 141.

[10] Dīpavaṁsa 1.14*ff.*

[11] Dīpavaṁsa 4.11, 18, 31, 32, 33, 54, 84, 88, 90; 5.28; 6.24, 29, 39, 43, 54.

with a magisterial disregard for chronology, means the Theravādins in the narrow sense (= Mahāvihāravāsin).

20 In this context the motive for placing the root schism before Aśoka is clear. If the schisms happened after Aśoka, then it would be impossible to assert that Aśoka was the specific patron of the Theravāda. He would have to be seen as the supporter of Buddhism in general. If the schism was in the time of Aśoka, this would contradict the triumphant message of Moggaliputtatissa's successful Third Council. The only solution is to put the schisms before Aśoka. Then the other schools are implicitly excluded from the narrative, and Aśoka becomes by default the special patron of the Theravāda.

3.1 The heresy of grammar

21 If we agree that the Dīpavaṁsa account of the schism cannot refer to the period immediately after the Second Council, can we establish when and in what context it really did originate? I think we can. To do this, we need to look more closely at the way the schism is actually described in the Dīpavaṁsa. It emphasizes the interpretative principles used at the Council:

22 Teachings metaphorical and definitive,
With meaning drawn out and with meaning to be drawn out,
Were elucidated by the Sutta experts.[12]

23 This verse is mockingly echoed in its account of the 'Mahāsaṅgīti' (Great Council) of the Vajjiputtakas:

24 Teachings metaphorical and definitive,
With meaning drawn out and with meaning to be drawn out,
Without understanding, those bhikkhus [confused].[13]

25 The Dīpavaṁsa goes on to explain (4.77) that the Vajjiputtakas (= Mahāsaṅghikas) confused the nouns, the genders, and so on. In short, they were

[12] Dīpavaṁsa 4.22: *Pariyāyadesitañcāpi atho nippariyāya desitaṁ/Nītathaññeva neyyathaṁ dīpiṁsu suttakovidā.*

[13] Dīpavaṁsa 4.73: *Pariyāya desitaṁ cāpi atho nippariyāya desitaṁ/Nītathaṁ ce'va neyyathaṁ ajānivāna bhikkhavo.*

grammatical heretics, whose foremost crime was bad writing. It would be unkind to linger on this point, but it is ironic that this accusation is made by the Dīpavaṁsa, perhaps the most badly written book in the Pali language.

26 Another crucial accusation is that the Vajjiputtakas/Mahāsaṅghikas revised the ancient texts, rejecting the Parivāra, the six books of the Abhidhamma,[14] the Paṭisambhidā, the Niddesa, some of the Jātakas, and some of the verses, and went on to compose others.[15] These works are all found in the Pali canon. Without exception, modern scholars are agreed that these works are late and are not *buddhavacana*. Thus the Mahāsaṅghikas may rightly claim to be the forerunners of an accurate historical-critical approach to Buddhist texts.

27 The Dīpavaṁsa's description of the rejected texts is a projection of the Mahāvihāra's dark side. Subconsciously, they know full well that these texts are late. The virulence of their attack—echoed elsewhere—demonstrates their fear of admitting this, and the concomitant need to externalize the problem. Why are they so afraid? Why not simply admit, as all the evidence would have it, that some of their texts are not *buddhavacana*? Admitting the inauthenticity of their own texts would destroy their own self-image as the true bastion of original, pure Buddhism. This would make nonsense of the ideology of Sri Lanka as the 'Dhammadīpa', and would ruin the Mahāvihāra's credibility in the competition for royal favours with the Abhayagiri. The fear is quite real: at some times the Mahāvihāra had to stand face to face with its own destruction. But the reality of the threat should not blind us to the illusions conjured in response to that threat.

28 The list of texts rejected is quite precise: 'some of the Jātakas', 'some of the verses'. As is well known, certain Jātakas form part of the early corpus of scriptures, while others were added continuously over many years. Similarly, many of the verses of the Khuddakanikāya are early, but many more are among the latest strata of additions to the canon.

29 In their current form, all these rejected texts are post-Aśokan. While the Abhidhamma project must have been underway in the time of Aśoka—as

[14] 'Six', because the seventh book, the Kathāvatthu, was not composed until the Third Council, which is later according to the Mahāvihāra's chronology.

[15] Dīpavaṁsa 4.76, 82.

suggested by Moggaliputtatissa's Abhidhamma connections and confirmed by substantial similarities among existing Abhidhamma texts—the texts as we know them were finalized later. Similarly, the Paṭisambhidāmagga is dated around 100 BCE.[16] The Niddesa applies Abhidhamma methodology to some early poems, and stems from a similar period. Thus we are firmly in the 'late canonical' period of the Mahāvihāra literature, and accordingly should look for the dispute in this period.

30 If we want to know who the Mahāvihāravāsins were arguing with, the Kathāvatthu commentary, though redacted later, is our main source of information. Overwhelmingly, this concerns disputes with the Andhakas,[17] a group of Mahāsaṅghika schools in the Andhra region, including Amarāvati, Nāgārjunikoṇḍa, etc. Thus we know that the Mahāvihāravāsins debated Abhidhamma extensively with the Andhakas, and it must surely follow that the Andhakas rejected the Mahāvihāra's Abhidhamma and related literature. But this is perhaps not of such great importance in itself, for it is probable that most of the Indic schools did not accept the Mahāvihāra Abhidhamma—in fact, they had probably hardly even heard of it. What matters is not so much that the Andhakas rejected these texts, but that the Mahāvihāravāsins knew they rejected them, and it hurt.

31 The Paṭisambhidāmagga and the Niddesa are also crucial here, in a different way. They are both included in the Khuddakanikāya, but each has strong affinities with the Abhidhamma. The *paṭisambhidās* were a minor doctrinal set for the early Suttas. The primary meaning relates skill at textual exegesis with penetration to the Dhamma: *dhamma* (text); *attha* (meaning); *nirutti* (language); *paṭibhāṇa* (eloquence, i.e. the ability of one who, knowing the text and its meaning, and being fluent in the ways of expression, to spontaneously give an accurate and inspiring teaching). The Paṭisambhidāmagga takes this occasional group and, stretching their application almost beyond recognition, develops the first distinctive Mahāvihāra 'Book of the Way'. As with all canonical Abhidhamma, the emphasis is on precise, clear cut doctrinal definition. Warder shows that the emphasis on this particular doctrinal category is peculiar to the Mahāvihāra.[18]

---

[16] ÑĀṆAMOḶI, *The Path of Discrimination*, xxxviii*ff.*

[17] About half of the disputes are with the Andhakas or their sub-schools.

[18] ÑĀṆAMOḶI, *Path of Discrimination*, introduction.

32 The Niddesas are similarly about textual exegesis. They are a pair of Abhidhamma style commentaries on the Khaggavisāṇa Sutta, Aṭṭhakavagga, and Pārāyanavagga, early poems subsequently compiled in the Sutta Nipāta. Their style is curiously Abhidhammic, in stark contrast with the casual, natural language of the texts on which they comment. In fact, they come across as an attempt to 'tame' some early texts which express doctrinal positions not easy to reconcile with the Mahāvihāra's developing stance.

33 As for the late Jātakas and verses, it would seem as if these were not so likely to be doctrinally controversial. They mainly deal with the Bodhisattva doctrine, which was emerging throughout all Buddhist schools, and if anything we would expect Mahāsaṅghika schools, such as the Andhakas, to be the forerunners in this movement. Nevertheless, the Kathāvatthu does record several controversies regarding the Bodhisattva and his career. The Andhakas asserted that the Bodhisattva was born as an animal or in hell of his free will (*issariyakāmakārikāhetu*),[19] which for them was an expression of his transcendent (*lokuttara*) nature, but which the Mahāvihāravāsins saw as a denial of the law of kamma. It is not sure whether the Mahāsaṅghikas rejected certain Jātakas and verses because of doctrinal problems such as these, or simply because they were extra-canonical.

34 Recalling the Dīpavaṁsa's accusations of bad textuality, I am struck by the aptness of a remark by Franklin Edgerton. Previously, Émile Senart had edited one of the most important and difficult works in the Mahāsaṅghika literature, the Mahāvastu, in the light of traditional Sanskrit and Pali forms. Edgerton commented that: 'Senart's extensive notes often let the reader perceive the despair which constantly threatened to overwhelm him.'[20] Following Edgerton's work, it is now generally acknowledged that the Mahāsaṅghika texts are written in a distinctively Mahāsaṅghika 'Hybrid Sanskrit', and are not just bad Sanskrit. But Senart's despair would echo the reaction of any Mahāvihāravāsin scholars, brought up on the simpler, cleaner Pali tradition, who confronted the Mahāsaṅghika texts. We therefore suggest that the Dīpavaṁsa's accusations of textual rejection and bad grammar were levelled specifically at the Mahāsaṅghika schools of Andhra,

---

[19] Kathāvatthu 622.

[20] Quoted in PREBISH, 'Śaikṣa-Dharmas Revisited', 191.

and by extension Sanskritic or 'modernized' Buddhism generally, such as the Abhayagiri.[21] In the usual mythic style, contemporary debates were backdated to give them a universal relevance.

35 There are other sources that also attribute the schisms to linguistic variation. For example, Vinītadeva gives this cause, and mentions the following language usages: Sarvāstivādins used Sanskrit; Mahāsaṅghikas used Prākrit; Saṁmitiyas used Apabhraṁśa; the Sthaviras (= Theravāda) used Paiśacī.[22] The Dīpavaṁsa's account must be seen in this light, that is, it highlights a primarily linguistic dispute. But the linguistic differences are merely a consequence of geographical dispersal. It is hardly possible that communities living in the same region would dispute over what language to use. The languages must have diverged as the schools spread over India and followed the Buddha's advice to teach the Dhamma in the local dialect.[23] Notice that the Sri Lankans did not follow this advice, and preserved the Dhamma in a foreign tongue, which they strenuously believed to be literally the language spoken by the Buddha.

36 The fact that the texts were not translated into Sinhalese indicates that they had attained a high degree of 'canonization' even before reaching the island. This tendency culminated in the later ideology of linguistic essentialism, where Pali was regarded as the 'root language of all beings'.[24] This means that one who had attained the *paṭisambhidās* would know through their own insight that *phassā* or *vedano* are incorrect nominative forms and that in the 'essence-language' (Pali) these should be *phasso* and *vedanā*. For the Pali school, the Mahāsaṅghika Hybrid Sanskrit was not a variant dialect, but a fundamental subversion of the Dhamma.

3.2 The Sri Lankan context

37 All this makes more sense when we consider the climate in which the Dīpavaṁsa and subsequent chronicles were composed. The events described close with the death of king Mahāsena about 304 CE, which follows

[21] Cf. Roth, lv.
[22] Pachow, 42.
[23] See Edgerton, 1–2; Lamotte, *History of Indian Buddhism*, 552–556.
[24] Ñāṇamoḷi, *Path of Purification*, 486–487 (XIV 25).

the the triumph of the Mahāvihāra over their bitter rivals the Abhayagiri monastery. This rivalry had started about 400 years earlier, when the Abhayagiri monastery was established by king Vaṭṭagāminī and became the home of Bahalamassutissa, the follower of a certain Mahātissa, who was expelled from the Mahāvihāra for inappropriate familiarity with layfolk. This monastery was subsequently regarded as schismatic from the Theravāda.[25] The Abhayagiri became associated with suspect teachings imported from the mainland. Since little if any of their literature survives, it is unclear exactly how their doctrinal position evolved.[26]

38 Both monasteries received royal support until the time of Vohārika Tissa, around 230 CE, when the Abhayagirivāsins were accused of introducing 'Vetulya' scriptures. It is usually presumed that these are Mahāyāna, though there is little direct evidence. In any case, these scriptures were suppressed. There is no discussion of the doctrines taught or why they are so dangerous. We might even be forgiven for wondering whether the actual contents of these texts were at all relevant.[27]

39 In any case, the 'Vetulya' books were burned and the bhikkhus disgraced. Following this, the kings Vohārikatissa, Goṭhābhaya, and Jeṭṭhatissa supported the Mahāvihāra. But the Abhayagiri continued to cause trouble. 60 bhikkhus were expelled by Goṭhābhaya for upholding the Vetullavāda; these are described in the Mahāvaṁsa as 'thorns in the conqueror's religion',[28] exactly as the Dīpavaṁsa called the Vajjiputtakas and other secessionists 'thorns on the banyan tree'. Much later, the Nikāyasaṅgraha of Dharmakīrti (14th century) was to turn this purely literary analogy into history, claiming that around 32 BCE, shortly after the Abhayagiri

---

[25] Mahāvaṁsa 33.99.

[26] There is a record in Samantapāsādikā 3.582 of a dispute over a point of Vinaya, which, in a remarkable reminder of the influence of the Aśokan precedent, was resolved by the king's minister. I cannot locate this passage in the Sudassanavinayavibhāsā, which may have an Abhayagiri connection.

[27] In the Cūḷavaṁsa (the later continuation of the Mahāvaṁsa) there is a story of a certain text called the 'Dhammadhātu', which was brought from India. (Cv 41.37*ff.*) The king, unable to discern what was right and wrong, enshrined it and worshipped it. The doctrines taught in the text are entirely beside the point: we are told that the king did not understand them. What was at stake was the ritual worship of the physical manuscript.

[28] Mahāvaṁsa 33.111: *vetullavādino bhikkhū, abhayagirinivāsino/ gāhayitvāsaṭṭhimatte, jinasāsanakaṇṭake.*

was established, a group of Vajjiputtaka bhikkhus, under the leadership of a certain Dharmaruci, came to Sri Lanka and, being rejected by the Mahāvihāra, found support in the Abhayagiri. These were the laxist Vajjiputtakas/Mahāsaṅghikas.[29]

40 But soon the tables turned. A bhikkhu called Saṅghamitta arrived from India. Painted in the darkest colours by the Mahāvihāravāsins, this monk helped the Abhayagiri to regroup. He was rejected by king Jeṭṭhatissa and fled back to India; but on the accession of Mahāsena he returned and performed the consecration ceremony for the king. Under Saṅghamitta's influence king Mahāsena persecuted the Mahāvihāra: the monks were driven from the monastery for nine years, and the Abhayagirivāsins, together with the evil minister Soṇa, stripped the Mahāvihāra of its treasures to adorn the Abhayagiri. Supporters of the Mahāvihāra were so appalled that a minister called Meghavaṇṇabhaya retreated to the Malaya region, where the Mahāvihāravāsins dwelt in exile, gathered an army and marched on the capital. But those were chivalrous days. The rebel minister reflected that he should not eat apart from his good friend the king, so on the eve of battle they shared a meal. The king asked why Meghavaṇṇabhaya was intent on war, and he answered that he could not bear to see the destruction of the Mahāvihāra. The king wisely asked forgiveness and pledged to rebuild the Mahāvihāra: an excellent example for those who would wage holy war today. But one of the king's wives was so grieved she had Saṅghamitta and Soṇa assassinated. The Abhayagiri was then stripped to adorn the Mahāvihāra.

41 These events culminated with the death of Mahāsena. The Mahāvaṁsa ends with the words: 'Thus did he gather to himself much merit and much guilt,' perfectly encapsulating the deeply ambiguous moral world of the Sri Lankan chronicles. Throughout we see a true devotion to the ideals of the Dhamma. While there is little evidence of advanced teachings and practices in the culture, still the kings make persistent efforts to live up to the ideals of the righteous king as represented by Aśoka. But the demands of government inevitably compromise these lofty ideals. Having closely

---

[29] LAMOTTE, *History of Indian Buddhism*, 371. Some modern writers (see PERERA, 37) connect these with the Vātsīputrīyas (Puggalavādins). This may not be wholly unjustified, since by the time of the Nikāyasaṅgraha there was not much clarity regarding these sects.

intertwined their conception of Buddhism with the Sri Lankan nation, the Sangha finds it impossible to retain an independence from the political arena. While we cannot approve of all we find within these bloodied pages, we must remember that history is like this, everywhere, all the time. On the whole Sri Lanka is no worse than any, and probably better than most. No doubt other Buddhist traditions faced bitter choices and deadly struggles. The difference is that we know nothing about them, as the Sinhalese are the only Buddhists of ancient India to preserve a historical literature. That literature asserts that without sometimes violent support Buddhism would not have survived. While we must deplore the violence, we cannot deny that the tradition, including the texts that tell us this story, has in fact survived where all others failed.

42 The Dīpavaṁsa and Mahāvaṁsa were formed in a desperate struggle. For the monks of the Mahāvihāra, the difference between sects was not a gentlemanly disagreement on points of Abhidhamma, but a battle for survival. The 'classical' phase of Mahāvihāravāsin literature—the chronicles and commentaries—were formed in the context of this struggle.

43 Of course this picture is one sided and melodramatic. Fa-xian, who spent two years in Sri Lanka a little after the events we have described, sees the Abhayagiri as the main monastery; it had 5000 monks, while the Mahāvihāra could only muster 3000. Characteristically, Fa-xian does not speak of any tension, but praises the beauty and devotion he witnesses in both monasteries. The combative spirit of the chronicles is as much a symptom of a frame of mind as it is the record of actual disputes.

44 There is something in these stories of the past that filled an urgent need for the Sangha in the present. The Mahāvihāravāsins, in those violent and intensely politicized times, needed an 'other'. This may be seen as an expression of the *vibhajjavāda* ideology, a need to separate oneself to create a sense of sacredness and purity. Throughout religious and magical thought, a ritualized physical separation is a source and a sustenance for holy power. The definition and identification of the 'other' is required in order to define and identify the 'self'. The need to demonize the 'other' hints at the dark side of the Mahāvihāravāsins: they are rejecting what they fear in themselves. We have already noted the ironies inherent within the Dīpavaṁsa: written atrociously, it accuses 'them' of bad textuality; and

while one of its central theses is a badly grafted foreign import, it accuses 'them' of introducing alien elements. We shall see in our discussion of the Śāriputraparipṛcchā that the Dīpavaṁsa is not alone in focussing on the mote in its brother's eye.

45 While these ironies may be quaint, even amusing, the same texts contain ironies of a far more dangerous sort. Most obvious is that, despite the tradition's insistence on preserving 'original' Buddhism unchanged, in fact the burden of the chronicles is to legitimize the fusing of the Church and State, a revolutionary innovation without precedent on the mainland. This is why so much stress is laid on the mythic reinvention of Aśoka as champion of the Mahāvihāra's brand of Buddhism. But going far beyond the example of Aśokan patronage of the Sangha or even interference in Sangha affairs, the chronicles pursue the politicization of Buddhism to its inevitable conclusion: the Buddhist justification of war. The Mahāvaṁsa depicts the guilt ridden king Duṭṭhagāmini returning from the battlefield and seeking solace from the Sangha for killing thousands of people in battle, just as Aśoka sought solace from Moggaliputtatissa for the murder of the Aśokārāma monks, or Ajātasattu sought solace from the Buddha for his murder of his father king Bimbisāra. The arahants reassure the king that he need not feel so bad, since he has really only killed one and a half people: one was keeping the five precepts, the half had taken refuge in the Triple Gem. The rest don't count.

46 Like all good myths, this passage is timeless; hence it has become central to the modern Sri Lankan Sangha's justification of war against the Tamils. Theravāda, while maintaining a quality textual tradition, in practice preserved neither more nor less of true Buddhism than any other school. But the stark contrast between the ideal monk as depicted in the early Suttas and the reality of Buddhism as lived created a tension on a deep level, a tension which is not resolved, but is projected on the 'other'.

47 It was king Parakkamabāhu I (1153–1186) who, in the midst of apparently endless military campaigns, finally reconciled the various Sangha fraternities. The Cūḷavaṁsa pointedly remarks that: 'despite the vast efforts made in every way by former kings down to the present day, the [bhikkhus] turned away in their demeanour from one another and took delight in

all kinds of strife'.[30] The analogy with the Aśokan Council is here made explicit: 'Even as the Ruler of Men Dhammāsoka with Moggaliputtatissa, so he [Parakkamabāhu] entrusted the grand Elder Mahākassapa ...'.[31] Following the Aśokan precedent, they gathered all the monks together, questioned them, solved the problems one by one, expelled the bad monks, and created a unified Sangha 'as it had been in the Buddha's time'.[32]

48 From these few examples—which could be expanded indefinitely—we can see how the Mahāvihāravāsin chronicles are built on a structure of repeating cycles, of recurring parallels. It becomes clear how the Dīpavaṁsa's depiction of the Mahāsaṅghikas as bad Vajjiputtaka monks is a mythic back-reading from the situation in the time of the Dīpavaṁsa. In myth time is uroboric, perennially swallowing its own tail: it is like this now, so it *must have been* like this then. The names and the details display a glinting surface of ever changing appearances, but the underlying patterns play themselves out with reassuring inevitability, like the changing of the seasons or the stars wheeling in the sky. The Sinhalese chronicles boldly meld the political and cultural history of their own people with the fundamental Buddhist myth, the life of the Buddha. Just as each ordination is a ritualized repetition of the Buddha's renunciation, making that remote act real in the present, so each event in the mythic structure informs the eternal now, the immanent sense of history lived as destiny. Thus the scapegoating and expulsion of the Vajjiputtakas becomes a catharsis required whenever the purity of the Sangha is imperilled.

3.3 Was Buddhaghosa a Theravādin?

49 The notion of purity of lineage is an essential element in the strategy of establishing a school of Buddhism. This is despite the fact that the very notion of *paramparā*, a particular ordination lineage, is absent from the early texts. Of course, it is not unreasonable to infer that they value a direct

[30] Cūḷavaṁsa 73.19. These events are also recorded in Parakkamabāhu's Galvihara inscription. See HALLISEY, 178.
[31] Cūḷavaṁsa 78.6.
[32] Cūḷavaṁsa 78.27.

connection of ordinations from teacher to student. But this can hardly be construed as central.

50 In the same way that Warder questioned whether Nāgārjuna was a Mahāyānist, it is possible to question whether Buddhaghosa, the 5th century compiler of the definitive Mahāvihāravāsin commentarial tradition, was a Theravādin in terms of his ordination lineage.

51 There is nothing explicit to go on. The later tradition asserted that he was born in Magadha, but this is a transparent effort to affirm his orthodox background. Interestingly, the Burmese maintain that Buddhaghosa was born in Burma. While few outside of Burma will find this plausible, this tradition implies that his ordination would be traced by the Burmese to the mission of Soṇa and Uttara to Suvaṇṇabhūmi. In other words, he came from one of the other missions, not from the mission that established the Mahāvihāra. From the later Burmese perspective of course this is all 'Theravāda', but in Buddhaghosa's day there was no unified form of Buddhism throughout Southeast Asia; in fact, many schools flourished in the region.

52 Since Buddhaghosa came from India, and given that the vast majority of Indian Buddhists were not affiliated with the Theravādins in the narrow sense required by the Dīpavaṁsa (= Mahāvihāravāsin), we may well wonder whether his ordination was really 'Theravādin'. He does mention having stayed in a few places on the mainland, some of which have been tentatively identified in Southern India: 'Mayūrasuttapaṭṭana' (Mylapore near Chennai); Kañcipura (Conjevaram near Chennai); and the postscript to the Visuddhimagga describes him as 'of Moraṇḍacetaka' (Andhra?).[33] However, the Mahāvaṁsa says he was born near Bodhgaya, although this is a much later tradition, attributed to Dharmakīrti of the 14th century. As far as his ordination goes, the Mahāvaṁsa could hardly be less specific: while wandering 'around India', he stayed at 'a monastery', where he met 'a teacher' called Revata, under whom he took ordination.[34] Revata is said to have taught the *pāḷi* of the Abhidhamma, but *pāḷi* here is used in its general sense of text and need not imply the Pali canon we know. Buddhaghosa apparently prepared a treatise called Ñāṇodaya, of which nothing is known,

---

[33] BUDDHAGHOSA, xvi.

[34] Mahāvaṁsa 37.216*ff.*

and an Aṭṭhasālinī, a commentary on the Dhammasaṅgaṇī. The existing commentary by Buddhaghosa on the Dhammasaṅgaṇī is indeed called the Aṭṭhasālinī, but it is not known if this had any relation to the earlier work, if indeed it ever existed.

53 When Buddhaghosa wanted to work on a *paritta* commentary, Revata told him that:

54 'Only the text (*pāḷi*) has been preserved,
There is no commentary here,
And similarly no Teacher's Doctrine:
That has fallen apart and is not found.'[35]

55 Revata then praises the purity of the commentarial tradition of Sri Lanka and encourages Buddhaghosa to go there and learn. This story is a legendary construct to emphasize the superiority of the Sri Lankan tradition; it is doubtful whether the Indians saw things quite the same way. Polemics aside, this tradition gives us no credible evidence that Buddhaghosa had an ordination in the Mahāvihāra tradition.

56 I take the example of Buddhaghosa only to make a rhetorical point. But it was normal for monks to travel around different monasteries, staying with different fraternities. This must have happened even more with the Abhayagiri monastery, who were said by the Mahāvihāravāsins to be accepting Indian monks of different traditions. But the Abhayagirivāsins were later fused with the Mahāvihāravāsins, despite this supposed impurity in their ordination lineage.

57 A similar situation must have obtained throughout Southeast Asian Buddhism, for we know that the areas of Thailand, Burma, and Cambodia where Theravāda now flourishes were formerly dominated by Mahāyāna, or Sanskritic Śrāvakayāna Buddhism. We note the widespread occurrence of the cult of Upagupta throughout this region, which is totally absent from Sri Lanka, and wonder whether this gives a hint as to the kind of Buddhism prevalent before the Theravāda orthodoxy. According to I-Tsing, in the lands on the eastern boundaries of India all four major schools flourished, while in the island regions the Mūlasarvāstivāda predominated.[36]

---

[35] Mahāvaṁsa 37.227.
[36] I-TSING, 9–10.

58 When these areas 'converted' to Theravāda (which mainly occurred around the 11th–12th centuries), it is impossible that all the monks took new ordinations. Of course, the official histories will assert that when the religion was reformed that all the monks conformed to the new system. But the practicalities of this are absurd: sending administrative monks from the city wandering through 1000s of miles of tiger-stalked, bandit-infested, ghost-haunted jungle tracks seeking out countless little villages, trying to persuade senior monks that their ordination is invalid or improper and must be done again, all on the basis of some political compromise in a far distant capital, in a region of ever shifting borders and allegiances. As history this is sheer fantasy, and the reality must have been that the reforms would directly affect only certain central monasteries. Others maybe used an informal procedure like a *daḷhikamma* (strengthening act), which is just an *ad hoc* procedure invented in lieu of doing a genuine *saṅghakamma*. But for the majority the reforms would have been irrelevant, even if they heard of them. It is only rational to conclude that the current 'Theravāda' lineage, like all others, must be a blend of many different strands.

59 Bizot's research in this area shows that the current situation in Theravāda in fact retains two distinct ordination styles.[37] One involves reciting the refuges once during the *pabbajjā*; in the other, the refuges are recited twice, once ending the words with the *anusvāra* -ṁ (pronounced -ng), and again with the labial nasal -m. The two statement *pabbajjā* has its roots in the ancient Mon Buddhism of the Dvāravatī period (7th–8th centuries), which was possibly introduced into Southeast Asia ('Suvaṇṇabhūmi') from southern India. Bizot believes that this two-statement *pabbajjā* was connected with certain esoteric meditation practices. The one-statement *pabbajjā* of the Mahāvihāra was introduced later, around the 14th–15th centuries, by monks who were in contact with Sri Lanka. But when the Sri Lankan lineage was re-established from Thailand, it was with the Mon two-statement *pabbajjā*. Meanwhile, the one-statement *pabbajjā* was progressively imposed on the Sangha in Southeast Asia, especially following the modernist Dhammayuttika reforms of Prince Mongkut in the 19th century. In one of those delicious ironies of history, the two-statement Mon

[37] My thanks to Rupert Gethin for this information.

pabbajjā now survives only in Sri Lanka, while the one-statement *pabbajjā* prevails throughout Southeast Asia.

60 The complexity of the situation is acknowledged by Somdet Ñāṇasaṁvara, the current Saṅgharāja of Thailand, in an important work Buddha Sāsana Vaṁsa. This discusses the modern Thai ordination lineage and the reforms introduced in the 19th century when the Dhammayuttika Nikāya was formed on the basis of the Burmese Mon tradition. It is believed that this tradition stems ultimately from the mission of Soṇa and Uttara to Suvaṇṇabhūmi in Aśoka's time. Here are some of Somdet Ñāṇasaṁvara's remarks:

> 61 'From the Buddha's Mahāparinibbāna until the present, more than 2000 years have passed, thus it is difficult to know whether the pure lineage has come down to us intact or not.' (16)
>
> 62 'If the lineage has faded away it is in no way harmful, just like Pukkusāti's[38] dedication to homelessness was harmless.' (18)
>
> 63 'The sasana in both countries [Sri Lanka and Suvaṇṇabhūmi] merged as one in that their lineage came from the same sasana that king Aśoka had sent from the capital at Pāṭaliputta.' (30)
>
> 64 [After the time of king Parakkamabāhu of Sri Lanka] 'Sri Lankan bhikkhus conferred with the Rāmañña [Mon] bhikkhus and were of the opinion that since the Sri Lankan bhikkhus were of the line of Soṇa and Uttara they were of the same communion.[39] The Elders thus invited one another to participate in *saṅghakamma* and together gave higher ordination.' (31)
>
> 65 [The lineages entered Thailand] 'many times through many periods ... as Buddhism entered the country in different periods, sects, and forms, it is difficult to know how they merged and how they declined.' (76)
>
> 66 [The Dhammayuttika Nikāya revitalized Thai Buddhism through] 're-establishing in Siam a direct lineage from Venerables Mahinda, Soṇa, and Uttara.' (77)

---

[38] This is in reference to the story of Pukkusāti in the Dhātuvibhaṅga Sutta, who went forth out of faith in the Buddha before formally receiving ordination. Ñāṇasaṁvara also mentions the going forth of Mahāpajāpati, the first nun, as a worthy precedent in this context.

[39] *Samānasaṁvāsa*, a Vinaya term meaning able to perform *saṅghakamma* together.

67 So while there sometimes appears to be an almost mystical belief in the inviolability of ordination lineages, saner voices are still to be found. No monk alive can guarantee his own ordination lineage. In this situation it is safer and more reasonable to focus on the way the holy life is lived rather than on unverifiable claims of a largely undocumented past.

Chapter 4

MONSTER OR SAINT?

I WOULD NOW LIKE TO LOOK at some of the northern accounts of the schisms, starting with the first division, the split into Sthaviras and Mahāsaṅghikas. The most prominent name is a certain Mahādeva.[1] For the Pali sources (including the Sudassanavinayavibhāsā), Mahādeva is one of the missionaries sent out by Moggaliputtatissa. He was one of the teachers[2] for Mahinda's going forth, and thus stands at the fountainhead of the Mahāvihāravāsin tradition.[3] Mahādeva is entrusted with the mission to Mahiṁsaka (Andhra?), where he taught the sutta on the Divine Messengers: 40 000 people penetrated the Dhamma, while a further 40 000 took ordi-

---

1 LAMOTTE (*History of Indian Buddhism*, 281) followed by NATTIER and PREBISH (213) mention a 'Bodhisattva Mahādeva', but this great king of the past, who developed the 4 *brahmavihāras*, and whose lineage was followed by 84 000 kings, is of course the well known Makhādeva of MN 83/MA 67/EA 50.4 and assorted Jātakas, etc.

2 The other teachers were Moggaliputtatissa and Majjhantika.

3 The account of Mahinda's going forth is similar in the Pali and Chinese, except the Pali says when ordained he became an arahant with *paṭisambhidās*, while the Chinese says he had the three knowledges and six *abhiññā*. (A similar variation is found in the description of Siggava and Caṇḍavajji at T24, № 1462, p. 678, b28–29, cf. Samantapāsādikā 1.36.) Just later, the Pali says he learnt the Dhamma-Vinaya as recited at the two Councils, 'together with the commentary', while the Chinese says he learnt the Sutta and Vinaya Piṭakas, memorizing the Tripiṭaka. (T24, № 1462, p. 682, a13–14) Both these changes may be seen as reflecting a Theravādin viewpoint: while the 3 knowledges and 6 *abhiññā* are standard, the *paṭisambhidās* are marginal in the Suttas and other schools, but were central to the Theravādin's root treatise the Paṭisambhidāmagga. The anachronistic mention of Mahinda memorizing the commentary needs no explanation.

nation. Frauwallner thinks of this region as the home of the Mahīśāsaka school, and suggests this originated as the result of this mission. Given the closeness of the Mahīśāsaka with the Mahāvihāravāsin tradition, this connection should come as no surprise.

2 There is also another Mahādeva. He too was said to live in Pāṭaliputta at the time of Aśoka. He too was a leader of a major group in the time of schisms. And he too is associated with the Andhra region. Given these striking correspondences, it might seem curious that the identification of the two is not taken for granted. Until we realize who this Mahādeva is: the reviled and despicable propounder of the 'five theses'; murderer of his father & mother, murderer of an arahant, provoker of the root schism that forever split the unified community of early Buddhism.

3 However, this lurid account, found in the Sarvāstivādin commentary the Mahāvibhāṣā, would seem to be struggling for historical support. In this chapter we'll review the main northern sources for their take on the first schism. In the next chapter we shall see how this relates to the supposed 'Mahādeva'.

4.1 Vasumitra's Samayabhedoparacanacakra

4 This famous and influential treatise on the origin of the schools was composed by a Sarvāstivādin Vasumitra. On doctrinal grounds it is dated as earlier than the Mahāvibhāṣā, probably around 500 AN (100 CE). The text exists today in three Chinese translations and one Tibetan.[4]

5 According to Vasumitra, about 100 years after the Nirvana (116 years according to Kumārajīva's translation), while Aśoka ruled in Pāṭaliputta, the Sangha was split into Mahāsaṅghika and Sthaviras due to the five theses. The five theses are supposed imperfections of an arahant, all of which would seem to be quite at variance with the perfection ascribed to the arahant in the early Suttas. But interpretation is all, so while the theses were obviously controversial, it is possible to read them as not being serious denigration of the arahant. They apply, perhaps, only to

[4] Partial translation at http://www.sacred-texts.com/journals/ia/18sb.htm. For discussion, see LIANG.

certain arahants, or are merely concerned with worldly things that are not essential to spiritual awakening.[5]

6 In Vasumitra and elsewhere the five theses are presented in a characteristic cryptic verse. Here is Paramārtha's version:

7 'Another person defiles the robes
Ignorance; doubt; and is led by another;
The holy path manifests through speech:
That is the Buddha's true teaching.'[6]

8 Various names are mentioned as supporting the five theses: Nāga (or Mahāraṭṭha in Paramārtha's translation), Pratyantika(?), Bahuśruta; and in two translations an extra name, perhaps Mahābhadra.[7] Mahādeva does not appear in either of the two earlier Chinese translations of Vasumitra, nor in the Tibetan translation.[8]

9 Only the last of the three Chinese translations, by Xuan-zang, mentions Mahādeva, saying: 'It is said to be due to the four assemblies not agreeing in their opinions of Mahādeva's five points.'[9] Lamotte suggests that this detail is interpolated from the Mahāvibhāṣā, which was also translated by Xuan-zang. This suggestion can be confirmed by a comparison of the verse summary of the heretical theses. This is character for character identical with the version (translated below) from the Mahāvibhāṣā. Xuan-zang translated the Mahāvibhāṣā in 656–659 CE and Vasumitra in 662 CE, so he must have copied his earlier rendering from the Mahāvibhāṣā into Vasumitra. This proves that Xuan-zang was influenced by the Mahāvibhāṣā in his translation of Vasumitra, and so we are justified in thinking that the insertion of Mahādeva was also an innovation of Xuan-zang, and was not in the Indic text.

10 It is rather a shame that, despite the fact that Lamotte has clearly demonstrated that this Mahādeva is a later interpolation in Vasumitra's treatise,

---

5 See WARDER, 209; COUSINS, 'The "Five Points" and the Origins of Buddhist Schools.'

6 餘人染污衣。 無明疑他度 。聖道言所顯。 是諸佛正教 (T49, № 2033, p. 20, a24–25). This verse has been reconstructed into Pali by COUSINS ('The "Five Points" and the Origins of Buddhist Schools', note 84): *parūpahāro aññāṇaṁ / kaṅkhā paravitāraṇā / dukkhāhāro ca maggaṅgaṁ / etaṁ buddhānusāsanaṁ* (or *buddhānasāsanaṁ*).

7 See http://sectsandsectarianism.santipada.org/thefirstmahasanghikas.

8 LAMOTTE, *History of Indian Buddhism*, 276.

9 謂因四眾共議大天五事不同 (T49, № 2031, p. 15, a20–21).

we still see references asserting that Vasumitra blamed the schism on Mahādeva.[10] This is no doubt due to Xuan-zang's prestige as a translator. It is an important point, for Mahādeva's name is smeared with the dung of scandal like no other, and the smell will linger as long as he is associated with the Mahāsaṅghika's origins.

11 All translations of Vasumitra speak of a later Mahādeva, and so we will henceforth distinguish Mahādeva I, the supposed schismatic, from this Mahādeva II. He was an ascetic of another religion who went forth in the Mahāsaṅghika 200 years after the Nirvana, and founded the Caitya sub-school.[11] Xuan-zang, having mentioned the first Mahādeva, says that 200 years later there was one who went forth, abandoning wrong and doing good, who was *also* called Mahādeva.[12] Thus he recognizes the two Mahādevas.

4.2 Bhavya's Nikāyabhedavibhaṅgavyakhyāna

12 Bhavya, or Bhāvaviveka, was a Madhyamaka philosopher of the 6th century CE. He records three accounts of the schisms, together with descriptions of the schools and their doctrines.[13] Bhavya I is the actual opinion of Bhavya and his teachers, while he records Bhavya II (Vibhajjavādin) and Bhavya III (Puggalavāda) for the sake of the record. He also includes a further tradition attributing the schisms to philosophical disputes, specifically the *sarvāstivādin* debate on the three times. Bhavya is writing at a great remove from the events, although no doubt he relies on earlier sources that are now lost to us.

13 The first list (Bhavya I) reproduces Vasumitra's list, with some small but significant changes.[14] It is usually regarded as of Sarvāstivādin origin, but unlike Vasumitra the first school mentioned is not the Sarvāstivāda but the Haimavata or the 'Original Sthaviras' ('Mūlasthaviras'). It is unlikely any

[10] E.g. NATTIER and PREBISH, 205; ROTH, vii; WALSER, 45; etc., etc.

[11] LAMOTTE, *History of Indian Buddhism*, 283.

[12] 有一出家外道。捨邪歸正。亦名大天 (T49, № 2031, p. 15, b1–2).

[13] mDo xc.12. Also known as the Tarkajvālā. Bhavya's life story at TĀRANĀTHA, 186–189. Translation in ROCKHILL, 182–196.

[14] The date is 160 AN, rather than Vasumitra's 100 or 116; however Bareau argues that 160 is just a confusion for 116.

school would call another group the 'Original Sthaviras', so this appellation must be the school's own self perception. Perhaps then Bhavya I should be seen as a Haimavata variation on Vasumitra.

14 Or perhaps it should be the other way around: Vasumitra is a Sarvāstivāda variation of Bhavya I. This is a radical hypothesis, for Bhavya was writing much later than Vasumitra. But Vasumitra also refers to the Haimavatas as the Mūlasthaviras.[15] Why should a Sarvastivādin writer call another group the 'Original Sthaviras'? In a natural sense, the Sthaviras who arose from the Mahāsaṅghika schism should be considered the 'Original Sthaviras'. But Vasumitra inserts the Sarvāstivādins at the head of his list while the Haimavatas are second, even though they are called the 'Original Sthaviras'. It is more natural to take Bhavya I as the original, making the list a Haimavata compilation, and Vasumitra a Sarvāstivādin rehash. If there is any truth to this, it is rather striking that our oldest epigraphic evidence for any school, even in its formative stage, is the Haimavata; and again in the Haimavata we see what might be the earliest form of the lists of schools.

15 Another peculiar feature of Bhavya I is that it gives a number of synonyms for the Sarvāstivādins: Hetuvādins (= Vasumitra), Muruntaka, and Vibhajjavādins. This clearly suggests that the Sarvāstivādins may also be called Vibhajjavādins; but when explaining these terms a little later, the same account defines Sarvāstivāda and Vibhajjavāda as in opposition. This curious state of affairs would only make sense if the original list emerged in a context where Sarvāstivāda = Vibhajjavāda, but the detailed explanations dated from a later time, when the two terms had come to mean opposing doctrines. Since the Sarvāstivādin's own texts treat the Vibhajjavādins as opponents, it is unlikely this identification could spring from them; hence this alternative name is absent from Vasumitra. The term Muruntaka is

[15] Xuan-zang: 二即本上座部。轉名雪山部 (T49, № 2031, p. 15, b10–11). But Paramārtha just has Sthavira 二雪山住部。亦名上座弟子部 (T49, № 2033, p. 20, b10). Kumārajīva has: 'One called Sarvāstivāda, also called Hetuvāda, Mūlasthavira school. The second is called Haimavata school (一名薩婆多。亦名因論先上座部。二名雪山部; T49, № 2032, p. 18, a24–25). Since both the other Chinese translations list two names for each of the Sarvāstivādins and the Haimavatas, whereas Kumārajīva has three for the Sarvāstivādins and only one for the Haimavatas, it seems that Kumārajīva has mistakenly assigned the Haimavata's alternative name, Mūlasthavira, to the Sarvāstivāda.

curious. Bhavya says it is 'those who live on Mount Muruntaka'. This is probably a reference to the famous Urumuṇḍa mountain near Mathura, known in Pali as Ahogaṅgapabbata. This mountain sheltered the renowned forest monasteries of the great (Mūla) Sarvāstivādin patriarchs Śāṇavāsin and Upagupta, and, as we shall discuss later, it was also the retreat resort of the Third Council patriarch, Moggaliputtatissa.

16 Bhavya's second list (Bhavya II) gives no information as to the date or cause of the schism, and merely lists the affiliation of the schools. It says the root schism is threefold: Sthavira, Mahāsaṅghika, and Vibhajjavādin. Cousin believes this must be a mainland Vibhajjavādin version, since it treats the Vibhajjavādins as one of the root schools. It would thus represent the Vibhajjavādin's own perception of themselves as a closely related group consisting of Mahīśāsaka, Kaśyapīya, Dharmaguptaka, and Tāṁraśātīya (=Mahāvihāravāsin?). Of course, if this theory is true, this would only serve as evidence for the late middle period (*circa* 400 CE), from when this passage evidently derives. We note that the mainland Vibhajjavādins may have seen themselves as forming such a group of schools, but such a perception is nowhere attested for the Mahāvihāravāsins, who saw themselves as radically alone.

17 The most important of Bhavya's lists is doubtless Bhavya III, which records the perspective of the Puggalavāda, which is not known from any source. This account is similar to Vasumitra's, but differs in many details. It says that 137 years after the Nirvana, under the kings Nanda and Mahāpadma (predecessors of Aśoka), there was an assembly of great monks at Pāṭaliputta: Mahākaśyapa, Mahāloma, Mahātyāga, Uttara, Revata, etc. Māra assumed the form of a monk called Bhadra and propounded the five theses. Later the 'very learned' (*bahuśruta*) Elders Nāga and Sāramati (or Sthiramati) adopted the five theses, resulting in the schism between the Mahāsaṅghika and the Sthaviras.[16] The name Nāga agrees with Vasumitra.[17] Bhadra might be the same as 大德 mentioned by Paramārtha and Xuan-zang. *Bahuśruta* also agrees with Vasumitra and possibly the Śāriputraparipṛcchā, although it's unsure whether it is a name or an adjective.

---

[16] LAMOTTE, *History of Indian Buddhism*, 281.

[17] It is perhaps worth noting that the Mahāsaṅghika Vinaya list of teachers also acknowledges a Nāga (尊者龍覺 T22, № 1425, p. 492, c22–23), while there is no Mahādeva. But this list is so long and dubious, and the name Nāga so common, that it counts for little.

18 102 years later the Mahāsaṅghikas split. Mahādeva, who was formerly an ascetic following another sect and lived on a mountain with a *cetiya*, rejected some basic Mahāsaṅghika tenets, and founded the Cetiya subschool of the Mahāsaṅghika (which was based in Andhra).[18] This is the only Mahādeva known to Bhavya, and is obviously Vasumitra's Mahādeva II. It should not escape notice that Bhavya's three lists represent the perspectives of several schools, and Mahādeva I has no part to play.

19 Bhavya III agrees with the Dīpavaṁsa in placing the first schism before Aśoka. This agreement in the general period of the schism has been taken by some scholars to show that these sources reinforce each other and hence have a genuine historical basis. But this is highly problematic. We have seen that the Dīpavaṁsa's dating of the schism is entirely useless, and no other source places the schism before Aśoka. There is no weight in the agreement of two sources if one of those sources is demonstrably wrong. Moreover, apart from the general period and the bare fact of the schism between the Sthaviras and Mahāsaṅghikas, the Dīpavaṁsa and Bhavya III have nothing in common: not the cause (textual revision vs. 5 theses); not the specific date (100 AN vs. 137 AN); not the place (Vesālī vs. Pāṭaliputta); not the king (Kāḷaśoka vs. Nanda and Mahāpadma); not the procedure (the Dīpavaṁsa depicts the Mahāsaṅghikas going off by themselves to do their texts, while Bhavya III depicts a conflict and split). We have to squeeze hard to extract any meaning out of the mere agreement in general period.

20 Bhavya III is comparable, not with the Dīpavaṁsa, but with Vasumitra. But the dating is just a source of confusion: Bhavya III is set in the reign of earlier kings, but due to the differences in dating the time between the Buddha and Aśoka, the calender date is later (137 AN vs. Vasumitra's 116 AN). None of this gives us confidence in relying on any of these dates.

21 Thus Bhavya III stands as an isolated account, which contradicts all other sources in many important details including the dating, and which was compiled centuries after the events: Bhavya was writing in the 6th century, and his source for this section probably dates around the 3rd–6th century.[19] The monks mentioned do not occur as a group anywhere else, and while some of the names are familiar, there is no supporting evidence for such

---

[18] Rockhill, 189.
[19] Cousins, 'On the Vibhajjavādins', 158.

a group. The mention of Bhadra being possessed by Māra gives sufficient evidence for the polemical nature of the account. Tāranātha alternatively describes him as so evil it was as if he was possessed by Māra.[20]

22 Bhavya III was not taken on its face value even within the Tibetan tradition. In the 17th century Tāranātha made an attempt to synthesize various sources including Bhavya and the Vaibhāśika account of Mahādeva. For him, Mahādeva came after Aśoka and Bhadra was one of Mahādeva's followers. Similarly the other monks mentioned in Bhavya's account above are located in the generations following Aśoka, when the heresy festered until resulting in schism in the time of a later Nanda. The reliability or otherwise of Tāranātha's version is not the point here, but it does give a precedent for questioning the chronology of Bhavya III.

23 We have seen that the Mahāvihāravāsin mythology paints a detailed enough background picture for us to discern their motives in placing the schism when they did. Below we shall see that the same applies to the Sarvāstivāda, and to some degree for the Mahāsaṅghika. But no legendary material survives from the Puggalavāda group of schools.[21] Thus there is no way of knowing why they placed the schism so early. But they must have had such an apologetic, responding to the universal human need to seek archaic authority for one's own spiritual tradition. In this case the crucial element in their story would have been to place the schism in the time of Nanda and Mahāpadma, thus (like the Mahāvihāravāsins) setting the scene to tell of their glorious triumph under Aśoka a few decades later.

4.3 Śāriputraparipṛcchā

24 The mythic character of this text is obvious. It is an aprocryphal Sutra of the Mahāsaṅghikas, which pretends to be a prediction of the future, but which, like all religious prophecy, is really about contemporary events. It was translated into Chinese towards the end of the Eastern Tsin dynasty (317–420 CE), and was probably composed a couple of centuries earlier than

---

[20] TĀRANĀTHA, 80.

[21] All we have is four treatises in Chinese translation: two similar Abhidhamma works (T № 1506, T № 1505), a discussion of their main doctrines (T № 1649), and a Vinaya summary (T № 1461). See CHÂU.

this.[22] We are tempted to describe it as a 'proto-Mahāyāna Vinaya-sutra', but this raises a number of issues: it is doubtful that the author thought of it in those terms, or whether he had even heard of the Mahāyāna. And is equally unsure whether it is to be dated earlier than the first Mahāyāna sutras; more likely it is roughly contemporary. A better description might be 'post-Āgama Vinayasutra'.[23]

25 The first passages feature the Buddha in dialogue with Sāriputta, who starts by praising the Buddha as one who teaches beings according to their inclination. A number of topics are raised: the nature of listening to Dhamma; the correct practice; drinking alcohol; food and lay people; king Bimbisāra is mentioned in this connection. The Buddha then says that he teaches according to the right time: 'When living at this time, one should practice according to this teaching; when living at that time, one should practice according to that teaching'.[24] Thus the text sets itself up for a story which from the point of view of the characters is in the 'future', but from the point of view of the author (and reader) is the past, whether real or imagined.[25] The Buddha then goes on:

> 26 'After I enter Parinibbana, Mahākassapa and the others should unite, so the bhikkhus and bhikkhunis can take them as their great refuge, just as [now they take] me, not different. Kassapa hands over to Ānanda. Ānanda hands over to Majjhantika. Majjhantika hands over to Śāṇavāsin. Śāṇavāsin hands over to Upagupta.
>
> 27 'After Upagupta there is the Mauryan king Aśoka,[26] a magnificent upholder of the Sutta-Vinaya in the world. His grandson is called Puṣyamitra. He acceeds to the throne ... [following is related the story of Puṣyamitra's devastating suppression of Buddhism, as translated in Lamotte, *History of Indian Buddhism*, pp. 389–390. Five hundred arahants were instructed by the Buddha not to enter Nibbana, but to stay in the human realm to protect the Dharma. When Puṣyamitra wanted to burn the texts of Sutta-Vinaya, Maitreya saved them and hid them in Tusita heaven.]

---

[22] 舍利弗問經 (T24, № 1465).

[23] In any case, it is obviously not a 'Mahāsaṅghika Abhidharma' as described in NATTIER and PREBISH, 207.

[24] 在此時中應行此語。在彼時中應行彼語 (T24, № 1465, p. 900, a10–11).

[25] This creates difficulties for the narrative time frame, especially in the Chinese, so I try to use the 'historical present'.

[26] 輸柯 *shu-ke* = Aśoka.

28 'That next king's nature is very good. Maitreya Bodhisattva creates 300 youths by transformation, who come down to the human realm to seek the Buddha's path. Following the 500 arahants' Dhamma instruction, men and women in this king's land again together take the going forth. Thus the bhikkhus and bhikkhunis return and thrive. The arahants go to the heaven realm and bring the Suttas and Vinaya back to the human realm.

29 'At that time there is a bhikkhu called *Bahuśruta,[27] who consults the arahants and the king, seeking to construct a pavilion for my Sutta-Vinaya, making a centre for educating those with problems.[28]

30 'At that time[29] there is an elder bhikkhu who desires fame, always anxious to argue his own thesis. He edits my Vinaya, making additions and expansions. The one established by Kassapa is called the 'Mahāsaṅghikavinaya'. Taking [other material] from outside and rearranging this with the remainder [of the original text], the beginners are deceived. They form separate parties, each discussing what was right and wrong.

31 'At that time there is a bhikkhu who seeks the king's judgement. The king gathers the two sections and prepares black and white tally sticks. He announces to the assembly: "If you prefer the old Vinaya, take a black stick. If you prefer the new Vinaya, take a white stick." At that time, those taking the black stick number 10 000, while only 100 take the white stick. The king considered that all [represented] the Buddha's words, but since their preferences differ they should not share a common dwelling. The majority who train in the old [Vinaya] are accordingly called the 'Mahāsaṅghika'. The minority who train in the new [Vinaya] are the Elders, so they are called the 'Sthaviras'. Also, Sthavira is made, the Sthavira school.[30]

---

[27] 總聞. A certain Bahuśruta is mentioned in Vasumitra as a leader of the three or four groups who discussed the five theses at Pāṭaliputta in the time of Aśoka. The first character here does not normally render *bahu*, but can stand for *sarva*, etc. While these stories are told of different eras, it may be that the names have been conflated, or perhaps are simply different people.

[28] 爲求學來難. An obscure phrase. Sasaki renders: 'As a result, it became difficult to come to study' (SASAKI 1998, 31, cf. note 43).

[29] 時. This is just a normal character representing the Pali '*atha kho* ...' or similar. While Lamotte and Prebish have declared the chronology of the Śāriputraparipṛcchā as incoherent, SASAKI (1998, 33) agrees that it straightforwardly sets the schism after Puṣyamitra.

[30] 爲他俾羅也。他俾羅部 (T24, № 1465, p. 900, b28). This is obscure; the text uses two terms for Sthavira, the translation 上座 and the transliteration 他俾羅.

32 '300 years after my passing away, from this dispute arises the Sarvāstivāda and the Vātsīputrīya [Puggalavādin]. From the Vātsīputrīyas arise the Dharmottarīya school, the Bhadrayānika school, the Saṁmitīya school, and the Ṣaṇṇagarika school. The Sarvāstivādin school gives rise to the Mahīśāsaka school, Moggaliputtatissa [or Moggali-upatissa; or Moggala-upadeśa][31] starts the Dharmaguptaka school, the Suvarṣaka school, and the Sthavira school. Again arises the Kaśyapīya school and Sautrantika school.

33 'In 400 years arises the Saṁkrāntika school. From the Mahāsaṅghika school, 200 years after my Nibbana, because of another thesis arises the Vyavahāra school, the Lokuttara school, Kukkulika, Bahuśrutaka, and Prajñaptivādin schools.

34 'In 300 years, because of differing education, from these 5 schools arise: Mahādeva school, the Caitaka school, the Uttara [śailas].[32] Thus there are many after a long period of decline. If it were not like this, there would only remain 5 schools, each flourishing.'

35 Here the schism is specifically attributed to a textual revision of the Vinaya. This has a striking resemblance to the crimes of Devadatta as described in the Mahāsaṅghika Vinaya. He is said to have striven for the splitting of the Sangha by composing new Vinaya rules and getting rid of the old. In addition, in the 9-fold *aṅgas* he composed different sentences, different words, different phrasing (味 = *vyañjana*), different meanings. Changing all the wordings, he taught each to follow his own recitation.[33]

36 This account of Devadatta's 'crimes' is not found elsewhere, and so we must have here a conscious recapitulation of a Mahāsaṅghika theme. It seems that at a certain stage the Mahāsaṅghikas became deeply worried with the changes being made in the Vinaya texts, and required a mythic authorization to condemn this process and reaffirm the integrity of their own tradition. As ever, the same evils recur in their cyclic inevitability, whether committed in the Buddha's day by Devadatta the root schismatic, or in latter days by the unnamed monk of the Śāriputraparipṛcchā. The great irony of the text is that, while it decries later additions to the Vinaya,

---

[31] 目揵羅優婆提舍 (*mu-qian-luo you-po-ti-she*) (T24, № 1465, p. 900, c3). The text is unclear, but seems to be saying that Moggaliputtatissa started only the Dharmaguptakas, although it might be read as implying he also started the Suvarṣakas and Sthaviras.

[32] 末多利

[33] T22, № 1425, p. 281, c12–21. Translation in WALSER, 100.

it is itself a later text that discusses and makes rulings on Vinaya. This reminds us of the irony of the Dīpavaṁsa criticizing bad grammar while using bad grammar, and criticizing textual accretions while itself including a northern interpolation.

37 One of the interesting features of the Śāriputraparipṛcchā is how it authorizes the Mahāsaṅghika lineage through the standard list of five Masters of the Dhamma. The Śariputraparipṛcchā is not alone in this, for the same list of patriarchs is preserved in Fa-xian's concluding remarks to his translation of the Mahāsaṅghika Vinaya, saying that only after Upagupta did the division into 5 schools occur.[34] It is therefore clear that Upagupta was an integral figure for the Mahāsaṅghika mythos, just as for the (Mūla) Sarvāstivādins. Since Upagupta was closely associated with Aśoka, this must mean that the schism was conceived as being post-Aśokan. This is not an arbitrary aberration of the Śāriputraparipṛcchā, but an intrinsic feature of its mythic structure.

38 It is also worth noticing that a pronounced strand of later traditions accepted the notion that the schism was post-Aśokan, and associated this with disputes among Upagupta's disciples. We have already noted this in the Tibetan historian Tāranātha. A Chinese example is Fa-yun, who says:

39 > Kassapa, Ānanda, Majjhantika, [Śāṇa]vāsin,[35] and Upagupta: those five masters, who penetrated the way with full powers, did not divide the teaching. However, Upagupta had five disciples who each held their own views. Later they divided the single great Vinayapiṭaka of the Tathāgata and founded five schools: Dharmagupta... Sarvāstivāda... Kaśyapīya... Mahīśāsaka... Vātsīputrīya... Mahāsaṅghikas.[36]

40 The list of patriarchs in the Śāriputraparipṛcchā is intended to invoke Upagupta's charisma on behalf of the Mahāsaṅghikas. While we mainly know of Upagupta from the (Mūla) Sarvāstivādin sources, this just reflects the quantity of these texts. There is no reason why the Mahāsaṅghika's claim on Upagupta should be any weaker than any other school.

41 This claim must have appeared in a time and place when Upagupta's fame and prestige was well established. Thus we should look to the North-

---

[34] T22, № 1425, p. 548, b10–15.

[35] 和修 is not Vasuki, as Lamotte and CBETA have it. Śāṇavāsin is commonly spelt 商那和修 e.g. T41, № 1822, p. 493, a12; T14, № 441, p. 310, c10–11; T46, № 1912, p. 146, a4.

[36] Fa-yun at T 2131, 4.1113 a22–b19, trans. LAMOTTE, *History of Indian Buddhism*, 176.

west, perhaps Mathura, and indeed we find the Mahāsaṅghikas attested there in an inscription on the Lion Capital in the 1st century CE.[37] According to Lamotte,[38] Mathura had several pro-Buddhist rulers during the Suṅga and Śaka periods, but not until the Kuṣāṇa period of the 2nd century CE did it become one of the main Buddhist centres. It is to this period that we should ascribe the creation of the great legends surrounding Upagupta and Mathura. We may suggest, then, that the Śāriputraparipṛcchā was compiled around this period in competition with the (Mūla) Sarvāstivādins, to assert their claim to be the true inheritors of the Upagupta lineage. This conclusion is however very tenuous, due to the paucity of the sources.

42 This dating of the Śāriputraparipṛcchā accords with the appearance in it of written texts. It must have been composed at a time when texts were written down; moreover, a sufficient period of time must have lapsed for it to have been forgotten that the old tradition was purely oral. The story of Maitreya hiding the texts in Tusita heaven irresistibly reminds us of the similar stories told of the Mahāyāna sutras. It is surely intended to raise faith in the transmission, but for us sceptical moderns it is more likely to do the opposite. It seems that this disappearance and reappearance of the texts was intended by the author of the Śāriputraparipṛcchā to set the scene for the disagreement over the texts. Read as history, it suggests that there was a period of disruption, and when the tradition was re-establishing itself, there was confusion about the exact state of the scriptures. This reminds us of the situation in Sri Lanka, where the Tipitaka was written down after a time of social upheaval.[39]

43 An intriguing question raised by the text is, what was the enlarged Vinaya? Of course, we do not know whether the events spoken of have any direct historical basis, or if there was, if any traces of the supposed enlarged Vinaya remain. Indeed all the Vinayas we possess have been

---

[37] LAMOTTE, *History of Indian Buddhism*, 525. Text at: http://gandhari.org/a_inscription.php?catid=CKI0048

[38] LAMOTTE, *History of Indian Buddhism*, 331.

[39] Although the Mahāvaṁsa itself says it was due to the 'decline of beings', whatever that means; it seems to refer to the general Buddhist notion of the deterioration of people's spiritual capacity.

enlarged to one degree or another, so it would seem futile to expect to find traces of the events in existing texts.[40]

44 The Śāriputraparipṛcchā speaks explicitly of a dispute over textual redaction, the mirror opposite of the Second Council, where the texts were held in common but the practices differed. There is no reason to suppose that such a dispute entailed any difference in Vinaya *practice*. There are many ways to expand a Vinaya text without affecting practice. For example, one could add extra Jātaka stories (as in the Mūlasarvāstivāda Vinaya), or supplements and summaries (as in the Mahāvihāra's Parivāra), or the reorganize the text around a master narrative (such as the Skandhakas of the Sthavira Vinayas).

45 Finally we note the obvious: that the Śāriputraparipṛcchā nowhere mentions Mahādeva. If he had really been the founding teacher of the Mahāsaṅghikas, it is unthinkable that any Mahāsaṅghika account of the schisms would have omitted him entirely.

4.4 Xuan-zang's Records of the Western Lands

46 The following account was told by Xuang-zang in his famous travel diary dated 646 CE. In Magadha, 100 years after the Nirvana, there were 500 arahants and 500 ordinary monks, all of whom Aśoka worshipped without making distinctions. One of the ordinary monks was Mahādeva, '... of broad and wide knowledge. In solitude he sought a true renown,[41] and with deep thought wrote a treatise, which however deviated from the Teachings ...'. He persuaded Aśoka to his cause, whereupon the good monks fled to Kaśmīr, refusing to return though Aśoka begged them. There is no mention of the Mahāsaṅghika or the five theses.[42]

---

[40] Nevertheless, I consider a few options in: http://sectsandsectarianism.santipada.org/sekhiyarulesreconsidered.

[41] 幽求名實. LAMOTTE renders this 'a subtle investigator of the Nāma-Rūpa (sic)' (LAMOTTE, *History of Indian Buddhism*, 280). But 實 means 'truth, actuality', and usually stands for such Indic words as *tattva*, *bhūta*, *satya*, *dravya*, *paramārtha*, etc. rather than *rūpa*. BEAL has: 'in his retirement he sought a true renown' (BEAL, 1983, 1.150), which is a sobering reminder of the flexibility with which Chinese can be rendered. After consultation with Rod Bucknell, I have followed Beal, although it depends on reading the text as 幽求實名.

[42] T51, № 2087, p. 886, b14.

47 The two divisions of the Sangha are of equal numbers, precluding the explanation (in the Mahāvibhāṣā and elsewhere) that the Mahāsaṅghika were so-called because they were the majority party. Cousins regards this explanation of the names Mahāsaṅghika and Sthavira as a 'myth based on a folk etymology. Clearly, the Mahāsaṅghikas are in fact a school claiming to follow the Vinaya of the original undivided Sangha, i.e. the *mahāsaṅgha*. Similarly the *theravāda* is simply the traditional teaching, i.e. the original teaching before it became divided into schools of thought.'[43]

48 Lamotte suggests that the description of Mahādeva sounds more like Sarvāstivāda than Mahāsaṅghika, although this is a tenuous inference, which moreover rests on the dubious interpretation of 名實 as *nāmarūpa*. The fact that his opponents fled to Kaśmīr should be enough to establish that Xuan-zang did not think of Mahādeva as Sarvāstivādin. As Lamotte notes, this is clearly a reference to the founding of the Sarvāstivāda in Kaśmīr, in flagrant contradiction with the normative account of the Kaśmir mission by Majjhantika, also recorded by Xuan-zang. Myth never allows mere consistency to get in the way of a good story.

49 The characteristic praise of Mahādeva's erudition is noteworthy, and may be a memory of the Vibhajjavādin missionary of the same name. It is only a short step to the opinions of Xuan-zang's student Kuei Chi.

4.5 Kuei Chi

50 Kuei Chi (632–682 CE) wrote that 'Mahādeva was a monk of great reputation and outstanding virtue, who realized the fruits while still young.' He was accused of the three sins and five theses because of jealousy.[44] Notice that Mahādeva is accused of three *ānantarika* sins. This is consistent with the main source for the 'evil' Mahādeva, the Sarvāstivādin Mahāvibhāṣā, to which we turn at last. Kuei Chi shows us that at no time was the scandal of Mahādeva accepted without question among those willing to inquire.

---

[43] COUSINS, 'The "Five Points" and the Origins of the Buddhist Schools', 57.

[44] 遂爲時俗所嫉 謗之以造三逆 加之以增五事 (T43, № 1829, p. 1, b3–4). The text gives a prose translation of the verse on the five points (T43, № 1829, p. 1, b4–5).

Chapter 5

THREE SINS & FIVE THESES

THE SARVĀSTIVĀDIN MAHĀVIBHĀṢĀ was compiled, according to legend, by a group of 500 arahants in Kaśmīr under King Kaniṣka; in fact it must have been after Kaniṣka and after the 2nd century CE. The creation of this magnificent commentarial edifice marked a bold attempt by the Kaśmīr branch of the Sarvāstivādins to establish themselves as the premier school of Buddhism following the patronage of Kaniṣka. The text devotes a lengthy section to explaining the 'five theses', following which it relates the story of Mahādeva.

2 Having already explained the 5 wrong views and their abandoning, then how do they say they arose? They say they arose because of Mahādeva.

3 In the past there was a merchant of Mathura. He had a beautiful young wife who gave birth to a son. His face was lovely, so they called him Mahādeva. Not long afterwards, the merchant took much wealth and went to a far country. There he engaged in trade for a long time without returning. When the son grew up he had indecent relations with his mother. Afterwards, hearing that his father was returning, his mind grew afraid. With his mother he formed a plan, then killed his father. Thus he committed one *ānantarika* sin.

4 That act gradually became known. So taking his mother they prepared to flee and hide in Pāṭaliputta. There he came across an arahant bhikkhu, who he had previously made offerings to in his own country. Again he was afraid his act would be revealed, and so he made a plan and killed that bhikkhu. Thus he committed a second *ānantarika* sin.

5 His mind became sad and worried. Later he saw his mother having intercourse with someone else. So in anger he said: 'For your sake I have already committed two grave sins. We have moved to another country, and still find no peace. Now you have given me up and pleasure yourself with another man! How can I endure such filthy deeds from you!' Thereupon in the same way he killed his mother. Thus he committed a third *ānantarika* sin.

6 But there was no cutting off of the power of wholesome roots for that reason, so he became gravely sorrowful and could not sleep at peace, [thinking]: 'How can one eradicate one's own grave sins?' He heard it rumoured that the ascetics, Sons of the Sakyan, taught a Dhamma for the eradication of past sins. Then he went to Kukkuṭārāma monastery. Outside the gates he saw one bhikkhu practicing walking meditation, chanting the following verse:

7 'If a man commits a heavy sin
By doing good, he makes it end
Then that man lights up the world
As the moon emerges from the clouds.'

8 When he heard this, his heart leapt for joy, knowing that by refuge in the Buddha's religion he would certainly end that sin. So he approached that bhikkhu and eagerly requested the going forth. Then that bhikkhu, when he saw him ask so confidently, gave him the going forth without questioning carefully. He allowed him to retain the name Mahādeva and gave him instruction.

9 Mahādeva was intelligent, so not long after going forth he could recite from memory the entire Tripitaka in its letter and meaning. His speech was clever and skilful, so he was able to instruct, and all in Pāṭaliputta without exception took him as their guide. The king heard of this and frequently summoned him within the palace, made offerings to him and asked for Dhamma instruction.

10 After leaving there, he went to stay in the monastery. Because of crooked thinking, in a dream he emitted impurity. However, previously he had been praised as an arahant. Then he asked one of his disciples to wash his soiled robe. The disciple said: 'An arahant has already eliminated all *āsavas*.[1] So how can the teacher now still allow this to happen?' Mahādeva replied: 'This is the troublemaking of Māra Devaputta, you should not think it strange. There are, in brief, two

[1] Lit. 'outflows' or 'influences'; a standard Buddhist term for mental defilements. The dialogue here puns between the literal and metaphorical meanings.

kinds of emission of *āsavas*. The first is the defilements. The second is [physical] impurity. The arahant has no defilement *āsavas*. But even they cannot avoid emitting the *āsavas* of impurities. For what reason? Although an arahant has ended all defilements, how could they not have substances such as tears, spittle, and so on? Moreover, all Māra Devaputtas are continually jealous and hating Buddhism. When they see someone practicing the good, they therefore approach to destroy them. They will even do this for arahants, which is why I emitted impurity. That is what happened, so now you should not have any cause for doubting.' That is called 'the arising of the first wrong view'.

11 Again that Mahādeva wished to instruct his disciples to delight in personal attachment [to him]. He falsely set up a system with a gradual explanation of the 4 fruits of asceticism. Then his disciple bowed and said: 'Arahants all have enlightenment wisdom. How can we all not know ourselves?' Then he replied thus: 'All arahants also have ignorance. You now should not lose faith in yourselves. It is said that all ignorance may be summarized as two kinds. The first is defiled; the arahant has none of this. The second is undefiled, which the arahant still has. Therefore you are not able to know yourself.' That is called 'the arising of the second wrong view'.

12 Then the disciples all went back and said: 'We have just heard that a noble one has already crossed over doubt. How is it that we still have doubt about the truth?' Then again he said: 'All arahants still have doubt. Doubt has two kinds. The first is the inherent tendency to doubt; the arahant has abandoned this. The second is doubt about the possible and impossible;[2] an arahant has not abandoned this. Even Pacceka Buddhas are similar in this regard to you disciples, although they cannot have doubt due to defilements regarding the truth. So why do you still despise yourselves?' That is called 'the arising of the third wrong view'.

13 After that the disciples read the Suttas, which said an arahant has the noble eye of wisdom, and can realize for oneself regarding one's own liberation. For this reason they said to their teacher: 'If we are arahants we should realize for ourselves. And so why [for example] does the teacher when entering the city not appear to have the intelligence to realize himself [what is the correct road to take]?' Then again he said: 'An arahant can still learn from another person, and is not able to know for himself. For example, Sāriputta was the

[2] 處非處 = *ṭhānaṭṭhāna*.

foremost in wisdom; Mahāmoggallāna was the foremost in psychic powers. But if the Buddha's [words] were not remembered, they could not know this for themselves.[3] This is a situation when one can learn from another and then oneself will know. Therefore regarding this you should not dispute.' That is called 'the arising of the fourth wrong view'.

14 But Mahādeva, even though he had committed a host of crimes, had not cut off and stopped all previous wholesome roots. Afterwards alone in the middle of the night his sin weighed heavily [thinking]: 'In what place will I experience all that severe suffering?' Depressed and afraid, he frequently cried out: 'Oh, what suffering!' His attendant disciple heard the cry and was amazed. In the morning he visited and questioned: 'How are you these days?' Mahādeva answered: 'I am extremely blissful.' The disciple questioned further: 'Last night did you cry out "Oh, what suffering!"' He then said: 'I shouted the noble path—you should not think this is strange. It is said that if one does not with complete sincerity invoke suffering summoning [one's whole] life, then the noble paths will not manifest. That is why last night I frequently cried out "Oh, what suffering!"' That is called 'the arising of the fifth wrong view'.

15 Afterwards, Mahādeva gathered and taught these 5 wrong views. He composed this verse:

16 'Another conveys [impurity to soil the robes];
Ignorance; doubt; he learns from another;
The path is caused by the utterance of a sound:
That is called the true Buddha's dispensation.'[4]

17 After that, the Elder bhikkhus in the Kukkuṭārāma monastery one by one passed away. On the 15th day, it came time for the *uposatha*.[5] In his turn Mahādeva took the seat for teaching the precepts. There he recited the verse that he had composed. At that time in the assembly there were trainees and adepts who were very learned, firm in precepts, and cultivators of jhana. When they heard that teaching, without exception they were alarmed and objected. They criticized that only a fool would make such a statement, saying: 'This is not

3 ? 佛若未記彼不自知 (T27, № 1545, p. 511, b18-19). SASAKI has: '... if the Buddha had not remarked upon their abilities, they would not have gained self-awareness.'

4 餘所誘無知　猶豫他令入　道因聲故起　是名眞佛教 (T27, № 1545, p. 511, c1–2).

5 The fortnightly recitation. It is through holding separate *uposathas* in the same monastic boundary that a formal schism can occur. But our text does *not* say this occurred.

found in the Tripitaka!' They immediately recomposed that saying thus:

18 'Another conveys [impurity to soil the robes];
Ignorance; doubt; he learns from another;
The path is caused by the utterance of a sound:
What you say is not the Buddha's dispensation!'

19 Then that whole night was full of rowdy arguments, until finally in the morning factions emerged. Within the city, the news spread until it reached the state minister. The matter gradually spread, and would not end. The king heard and personally went to the monastery, but each faction stuck to its own recitation. Then the king, hearing this, himself began to doubt. He questioned Mahādeva: 'Which side should we now trust?' Mahādeva said to the king: 'In the precept scriptures it says in order to settle issues, one should rely on what the majority say.' The king then instructed both factions of the Sangha to stand apart. The noble faction, though many in years, were few in number. Mahādeva's faction, though few in years, were many in number. The king then trusted Mahādeva's group, since they were the majority, and suppressed the other group. When this was completed he returned to the palace.

20 At that time, in the Kukkuṭārāma monastery there was still open unextinguished argument with those of other views, until there was a division into two sections: first was the Sthavira school;[6] second was the Mahāsaṅghika school.

21 At that time all the noble ones, knowing that the community was rebellious, left the Kukkuṭārāma monastery, wishing to go elsewhere. When the ministers heard that, they immediately told the king. The king, hearing this, was angry, and commanded his ministers: 'Take them all down to the Ganges riverfront. Put them in a broken boat and float them in midstream to drown. Then we'll find out who is a noble one, and who is an ordinary person!' The minister respectfully carried out the king's command and put it into effect. Then all the noble ones arose with psychic powers, just like a king goose flying in the air, and they left. Returning, they used their psychic power to grab those in the boats who they had left the Kukkuṭārāma monastery with, and who did not have psychic powers. Displaying many miracles, they manifested in various forms. Then they voyaged through the sky to the north-west and left.

[6] Not Sarvāstivāda as claimed by NATTIER and PREBISH, 201.

22 When the king heard and saw this he was deeply regretful. He fainted and fell down on the ground. They sprinkled him with water, and only then did he regain his senses. Quickly he sent out scouts to follow [the arahants] where they went. A minister returned having found out they were staying in Kaśmīr. But when the Sangha was asked to return, all refused the insistent request. The king then gave away all Kaśmīr, establishing a monastery for the noble ones to stay. Each monastery was named after the various altered forms that each had previously manifested [when fleeing]. It is said that there were 500 'Pigeon Monasteries'. Again he sent a messenger with much wealth to organize for their material needs and offerings. Because of this, that land up until the present has had many noble beings upholding the Buddha's Dhamma, which has been handed down from then until now and is still flourishing.

23 After the king of Pāṭaliputta had already lost that community, leading others he went to make offerings to the Sangha at the Kukkuṭārāma monastery.

24 Afterwards, Mahādeva occasionally went into the city, where there was a soothsayer. [Mahādeva] met him; [the soothsayer] saw him, and secretly predicted that:[7] 'Now this Son of the Śakyan will surely die after seven days.' When [Mahādeva's] disciples heard, they became depressed and spoke [to Mahādeva]. He replied: 'I have known this for a long time.' Then he returned to Kukkuṭārāma monastery and dispatched his disciples to spread out and tell the king and all wealthy householders of Pāṭaliputta: 'After seven days retreat I will enter Nibbana.' When they heard, the king and all without exception began to lament.

25 When the seventh day was reached, his life came to an end. The king and all the citizens were full of grief and regret. They brought fragrant firewood, together with many oils, flowers and offerings. They piled them in one place to burn them. But when they brought the fire there, it went out. Many times they tried in different ways, but just could not make it burn. It is said that a soothsayer said to the people: 'This will not burn with these good quality cremation materials. We should use dogshit and smear filth.' After following this advice, the fire immediately blazed up, instantly burning up and becoming ashes. A strong wind blew up and scattered the remains.

---

[7] ？遇爾見之竊記彼言

> This was because he had earlier originated those wrong views. All those with wisdom should know to dispel them.[8]

26 This account is found only in the great Mahāvibhāṣā (T 1545) and not in Buddhavarman's earlier Vibhāṣā translation (T 1546).[9] But who could resist such a lurid tale? This became the definitive version, and was further elaborated, e.g. by Paramārtha in the sixth century, and taken up by most later Chinese accounts.

27 There are a number of points to be made here. First we notice that the text is explicitly presented as an addendum to the basic discussion of the 5 points. Next we see that the story appears to have sprung into being as a full fledged myth of origins. Like any myth, it probably derives from a number of sources. Lamotte sees the Aśokavadāna's tale of a corrupt monk in the time of Upagupta as a likely source.[10] In fact most of the elements of the Mahāvibhāṣā's story could be assembled from already existing elements available to the Kaśmīr authors: the tales of Upagupta and the unnamed bad monk from the Aśokavadāna giving the narrative context; the Vibhajjavādin inheritance shared with the Kathāvatthu on the five points, in substance and sequence; Vasumitra for the basic details of the schism. These are blended with a good dose of literary flourish, myth, and satire: Mahādeva's funeral is a parody of the Buddha's funeral.

28 The remaining detail that I cannot account for from Indic sources is the motif of the murder of the father by the son who is sleeping with the mother. This is not found, so far as I am aware, in any earlier Indic myths. We note that Kaśmīr had been under Greek influence and sometimes rulership for several centuries before the compilation of the Mahāvibhāṣā, and that there are several references in Greek sources to the performance of Greek drama in Asia. Greek theatres have been unearthed in nearby Bactria, but not yet in Kaśmīr.[11] The possibility holds that this 'Oedipal' motif arose from Greek influence.

---

[8] T27, № 1545, p. 510, c23–p. 512, a19. In several places I have referred to LIANG's partial translation of this passage, as well as SASAKI, "Buddhist Sects in the Aśoka Period. (7) The Vibhāṣā and the Śāriputraparipṛcchā", 12–19.

[9] LAMOTTE, *History of Indian Buddhism*, 278.

[10] LAMOTTE, *History of Indian Buddhism*, 277.

[11] MCEVILLEY, 386–388.

29 While the king is not named, it seems probable that it was Aśoka. The text is speaking from the same tradition as Vasumitra, and regardless of whether the 'Vasumitra' of the treatise was the same as the 'Vasumitra' associated with the redaction of the Mahāvibhāṣā, it would seem unlikely that the extremely learned authors of the Mahāvibhāṣā were unaware of Vasumitra's account. Hence following Vasumitra they probably associated these events with Aśoka.

30 The content of the passage supports this chronology. As far as we know, Aśoka is the only king of Pāṭaliputta explicitly associated with missions to Kaśmīr. Furthermore, he is represented as donating all Kaśmīr, and, pious exaggeration aside, Aśoka was perhaps the only king of Pāṭaliputta whose sway extended so far. The reason for the omission of his name is not hard to find. The passage is presented as a retelling of a story from another source. Presumably in its original context the identity of the king was clear and the authors of the Mahāvibhāṣā probably assumed this would be understood. Nevertheless, even though we may concur with ascribing this episode to the reign of Aśoka, the fact that the text does not specify the time means that it cannot serve as an independent evidence in favor of Vasumitra's chronology.

31 Despite the king's temporary anger, he soon relented and established monasteries throughout Kaśmīr, while those (Mahāsaṅghikas) who remained in the old lands were corrupt and worthless. While we should never take such polemics too seriously, there may be a degree of truth in the vitriol, for it is normal that long established traditions, especially with royal sponsorship, tend to become decadent, and reform movements have more chance to live, experiment, and grow in the outer regions.

32 The story's description of how the five theses came to be formulated has the ring of reality. In my experience, it is common that when monks live close to a great teacher, they will usually believe he is an arahant, and inevitably questions arise as to conduct. Some random examples that I have heard in my time as a monk: Can an arahant smoke? Can an arahant walk into the hall patting a dog and forget to wipe his feet? Can an arahant cry during a Dhamma talk? Can an arahant announce his attainment—on TV? Can an arahant suffer from Alzheimer's? Can an arahant express support for a politician who turns out to be grossly corrupt? And not least—can an

arahant have wet dreams? These arise in the kind of real life context that is depicted in the Mahāvibhāṣā's story of Mahādeva. This is perfectly in line with how similar questions are treated in the Suttas:

> 33 'Here, Sandaka, some teacher claims to be omniscient and all seeing, to have complete knowledge and vision thus: "Whether I am walking or standing or sleeping or awake, knowledge and vision are continuously and uninterruptedly present to me." He enters an empty house, he gets no alms food, a dog bites him, he meets with a wild elephant, a wild horse, a wild bull, he asks the name and clan of a woman or a man, he asks the name of a village or a town, and the way to go there. When he is questioned "How is this?" he replies: "I had to enter an empty house, that is why I entered it. I had to get no alms food, that is why I did not get any. I had to be bitten by a dog ... I had to meet a wild elephant, a wild horse, a wild bull ... I had to ask the name ... I had to ask the way to go there, that is why I asked." '[12]

34 Such situations would have been as common in ancient India as they are today, and the Mahāvibhāṣā's account realistically shows how such questions could have arisen in the context of the five points.

35 The story behind points 2–4, dealing with the kind of knowledge an arahant should have, also seem to me to be a realistic context. Mahādeva sets up a system whereby he can assess and guarantee the attainments of his disciples, making Mahādeva and his students dependent on each other in a sort of mutual ego massage. This kind of symbiotic teacher/student relationship is common in spiritual circles, and it is also common in modern Buddhism that this would be accompanied by a system which verifies various attainments of concentration or wisdom. Not infrequently, the students themselves do indeed doubt such claims: I myself have been in this situation. The whole context calls into question the belief that the five theses are intended to be a criticism of the arahant. This interpretation has already been questioned by Cousins on the basis of the Kathāvatthu, who argues that what is criticized is certain kinds of arahants, namely those without psychic powers. Mahādeva himself is supposed to be an arahant; given his character in the story, it could hardly be the case that he is criticizing himself. Nor is he criticizing his followers. He is merely pointing out that arahantship is not omniscience, but relates solely to liberating

---

[12] MN 76.21, translation BODHI/ÑĀṆAMOḶI. See ANĀLAYO.

spiritual knowledge. While one may or may not agree with his particular interpretations, this general position is no different from any other Buddhist school. It is often suggested that the five theses paved the way for the emergence of the Bodhisattva ideal and the later idea of the 'selfish arahant'. While there may be something to this, there is no hint of such developments at this stage. The real issue was not a theoretical problem with arahantship, but the misuse of spiritual authority. Compliance with an externally assessed system, rather than inner realization, becomes the standard by which spiritual growth is measured.

36 Mahādeva first proclaimed his heretical teachings in the form of a verse recited after the fortnightly recitation of the *pāṭimokkha*. It is the custom of bhikkhus and bhikkhunis to come together every fortnight to recite the monastic code. In the Mahāpadāna Sutta this recitation—though in the context of a past Buddha—was the verses known as the 'Ovāda Pāṭimokkha'. These verses may have formed the first *pāṭimokkha*. In any case, it remained—and still does remain—the custom of the Sangha to accompany the dry list of Vinaya rules with some verses of inspiration, typically the 'Ovāda Pāṭimokkha'.[13] Some of these verses end with the famous declaration that: 'This is the dispensation of the Buddhas', and these particular verses are in fact found in the Sanskrit *pāṭimokkha* text of the Mahāsaṅghika and the Sarvāstivāda.

37 Now, this phrase is also found in Mahādeva's heretical verses above, where he claims that his 5 theses are 'the teaching of the Buddhas'. It seems that he was recasting in his own form the Ovāda Pāṭimokkha verse that was regularly recited at the *uposatha*. One of the Ovāda Pāṭimokkha verses that ends with 'This is the dispensation of the Buddhas' starts with the phrase: *Anūpavādo, anūpaghāto* (Sarv: *(nopavā)d(ī) nopaghātī*; Mahāsaṅghika *āropavādī aparopaghātī*). *Anūpavādo* is identical in rhythm and similar in sound to *parūpahāro*, the Pali term meaning 'conveyance by another', which appears to start off Mahādeva's verse. But *parūpahāro* (literally 'other-close-bring') is hardly a clear description of what the first of the 5 theses is about. However the use of such an obscure term would make sense if it was originally composed for the role it plays in the Mahāvibhāṣā: to substitute as closely as possible to the well known verses recited at the *uposatha*.

---

[13] PACHOW, 192–197.

38 Mahādeva is accused of committing only three *ānantarika* acts. These are carefully counted, and the number is repeated elsewhere. An *ānantarika* act is one of the most heinous crimes known in Buddhism, resulting in unavoidable rebirth in hell. But the list of *ānantarika* acts is well known and standard, and consists of five. The two not mentioned in the Mahāvibhāṣā's account are the malicious shedding of the Buddha's blood—which, to state the obvious, is not possible after the Buddha's death—and causing a schism in the Sangha. Mahādeva, though often taken to be the root schismatic, is not accused, even in the texts that want to destroy his name forever, of deliberately and maliciously causing a schism in the technical sense required by the Vinaya. Thus the traditions did not regard the Mahāsaṅghika split, regrettable as it was, as a schism.

39 The Mahāvibhāṣā obviously did not refrain from accusing Mahādeva of causing schism out of any sense of tender affection. Why then did it not make this accusation? The authors of the Mahāvibhāṣā were learned monks fully versed in the Vinaya. To them it would have been obvious that it was technically impossible for Mahādeva to cause a schism in the Sangha. The Vinaya states that a formal schism cannot be caused by a lay person or even a novice, but only by a fully ordained bhikkhu. But Mahādeva had committed three *ānantarika* sins, rendering it impossible for him to ordain as a bhikkhu. The text is quite aware of this, which is why it takes care to note that his ordination teacher did not question carefully, as he is required to do in the Vinaya. Thus his ordination was invalid, and he could not have caused a schism.[14]

5.1 Which Mahādeva?

40 We have seen that Bhavya, Vasumitra, and the Śāripūtraparipṛcchā, none of whom mention the original Mahādeva, all mention the later Mahādeva II, a few generations after Aśoka. He is associated with the formation of the later Mahāsaṅghika branches in Andhra. Bhavya[15] and Vasumitra[16]

[14] See SASAKI, "Buddhist Sects in the Aśoka Period. (7) The Vibhāṣā and the Śāriputraparipṛcchā", 30.

[15] ROCKHILL, 189.

[16] 有一出家外道。捨邪歸正。亦名大天 (T49, № 2031, p. 15, b1–2).

specify that Mahādeva II was an ascetic converted from another sect, which does not agree with the story of Mahādeva I.

41 Lamotte argues against the identification of the good Mahādeva of the Pali tradition with the Mahāsaṅghika Mahādeva on two grounds. His minor reason is the geographical argument: Mahādeva the *vibhajjavādin* is sent to Mahiṁsaka, while Mahādeva the later Mahāsaṅghika reformer is in Andhra. Lamotte dismisses as 'vain'[17] attempts to locate Mahiṁsaka in Andhra, but later he more moderately says it is 'possible'.[18] Certainly, the canonical Pali sources[19] locate a 'Mahissati' near Ujjeni in Avanti. But the Pali commentaries locate Mahiṁsaka in Andhra.[20] The inscriptions confirm that the Mahāvihāra had a branch or branches in Andhra, and indeed there are references to the 'Andhra Commentary', so we can assume that they knew what they were talking about, and that the Pali commentarial sources think of Mahiṁsaka as Andhra, regardless of what other sources may say. Indeed, there are several inscriptions referring to the Mahīśāsakas in Andhra, and inscriptions in Andhra region that refer to the 'Ruler of Kaliga and Mahisaka'. About 200 kms to the Southwest of Nāgārjunikoṇḍa there is a reference to Mahiṣa-visaya.[21] I would therefore suggest we have reasonable grounds for assuming that Mahiṁsaka can be Andhra, at least from the Sri Lankan point of view.

42 More important is the doctrinal problem: how could Moggaliputtatissa, an avowed Vibhajjavādin, have associated with a heretic like Mahādeva? But the evidence for Mahādeva's heresy is thin indeed. The whole story is based on the Mahāvibhāṣā, written 400 or more years after the events. And—this might seem pedantic, but it is an important point—Moggaliputtatissa is not 'an avowed Vibhajjavādin'. While he may have thought of himself as belonging to a school called Vibhajjavāda, the evidence does not make this explicit. Rather, he said the Buddha was a Vibhajjavādin, probably opposing the heretical teachers of a 'self', which was not a Mahāsaṅghika doctrine or anywhere imputed to Mahādeva.

---

17 LAMOTTE, *History of Indian Buddhism*, 299.

18 LAMOTTE, *History of Indian Buddhism*, 342.

19 Dīgha Nikāya ii 235; Sutta Nipāta 1017.

20 COUSINS, 'On the Vibhajjavādins' 161, refers to Vjb 28: *Mahiṁsakamaṇḍala Andharaṭṭhanti vadanti ...*

21 COUSINS, 'On the Vibhajjavādins', 166.

43 In the end I am inclined to accept two Mahādevas. The first lived at the time of Aśoka, was one of Mahinda's teachers, and went on a mission to Mahiṁsaka (= Andhra), where he became a leading figure in the formation of the Mahīśāsaka school. The second lived a couple of hundred years later in the same area, and was a local leader of one of the subsects of the Mahāsaṅghikas. Neither had anything to do with the original schism or the five theses.[22] The similarities of the names and areas of activity led to their conflation, and the story of the corrupt unnamed monk from the Aśokavadāna was incorporated to explain how the most orthodox school—from the Sarvāstivādin point of view, i.e. themselves—came to be relocated away from the power centre of original Buddhism.

44 One further point to consider: if Mahādeva was not originally associated with the five heresies, why was his name singled out? One reason could be the similarities in names and locations with the one or two other Mahādevas. But we might also ask, who else in Buddhism is reviled in this way? There is only one monk in Buddhist history whose name comes in for such treatment: Devadatta. He was closely associated with Ajātasattu, king of Magadha, just as Mahādeva was associated with Aśoka. And Devadatta also proposed a set of 'five theses' in order to provoke a schism. There is a lot of mythic assimilation going on between these two pairs. Without wishing to linger on this point, I would raise the question whether Mahādeva fits the evil role simply because his name is similar to Devadatta.

5.2 The five heresies

45 The usual list of five theses is:

- That semen may be conveyed to an arahant (by non-human beings while he is asleep).
- That an arahant may have doubt.
- That an arahant may have ignorance.
- That an arahant may be led to comprehension by others.
- That the path may be aroused by crying 'Aho! What suffering!'

46 The middle three dealing with the 'imperfections' of the arahant's knowledge are treated quite briefly and repetitiously in the Kathāvatthu; the

[22] See http://sectsandsectarianism.santipada.org/dhammaorvinaya.

commentary treats them synoptically. The Kathāvatthu stresses the knowledge and wisdom of an arahant and has the opponent agree that the arahant does not lack knowledge regarding Dhamma. This goes on for some time, but the text is tantalizingly brief in addressing the actual point. The opponent asks: 'May not an arahant be ignorant of the name and lineage of a woman or a man, of a right and wrong road, or of the names of grasses, twigs, and forest plants?' This reminds us of Mahādeva's claim that an arahant might not have personal knowledge about Sāriputta and Moggallāna, i.e. incidental or historical details. This is entirely reasonable, and no Theravādin would dispute it. The issue is whether this kind of 'unknowing' has anything to do with 'ignorance' in the spiritual sense. But the responder does not make this explicit, merely adding: 'Would an arahant lack knowledge of the fruit of stream-entry, once-return, non-return, and arahantship?'—'That should not be said ...'. Despite the obscure phrasing, the point is clear enough, that an arahant might doubt about worldly matters, but not about matters of spiritual significance. Thus the whole question seems to be more a matter of terminology than different worldviews.

47 The opponent introduces the distinction between an arahant who is 'skilled in their own Dhammas' and type who is 'skilled in another's Dhammas'. The commentary aligns the first with one 'released by wisdom', who is skilled in his 'own dhamma' of arahantship, the second also is 'both ways released', being also proficient in the eight attainments. It would perhaps be more plausible to see this as the distinction between an one who knows his own mind (as in the Satipaṭṭhāna Sutta) and one who reads other's minds (as in the Gradual Training, e.g. Sāmaññaphala Sutta, etc.). Be that as it may, the Mahāvihāravāsin commentary, even while insisting on the unimpeachablility of the arahant, is developing the conceptual framework that would eventuate in a significant erosion of the arahant's status. The ultimate outcome of this process would be the belief, normative in modern Theravāda, that an arahant might not attain jhana.

48 Given that the middle three theses are not that weighty, the more controversial views are the first and last. The last is that one can give rise to the path through wailing 'O, suffering'. I will not discuss this here,[23] but there is one interesting detail in the Kathāvatthu's discussion. It says that

---

[23] Kathāvatthu 2.6.

if this were the case, then one who had murdered their mother, father, or arahants, spilled the Buddha's blood or caused schism in the Sangha could arouse the path merely by uttering 'O suffering!'[24] This rather overstates the case, for the proposition would seem to be that crying 'O suffering' was one condition for the path, not in itself sufficient. In any case, we notice that these crimes are almost identical with the crimes actually attributed to Mahādeva in the Mahāvibhāṣā. The list is of course stock, so perhaps we should make nothing of it. But it is possible that a similar argument was known to the Sarvāstivādins, who gave the accusations flesh and blood by pinning them on Mahādeva.

5.3 'Outflows'

49 But the most interesting, and probably decisive, consideration is whether an arahant can emit semen. The idea is expressed in different ways, probably partly due to the obscure nature of the summary verse in which the 5 theses are expressed, and partly due to a futile attempt at discretion. But the basic idea is that an emission need not be a matter of mental defilement. The 'conveyance' is evidently the conveyance of the semen to the arahant by non-human beings, especially those associated with Māra.

50 While this idea seems bizarre to us, it has substantial correlations in early thought. The notorious *Malleus Maleficarum* alleges that unclean devils such as *incubi* and *succubi* ' ... busy themselves by interfering with the process of normal copulation and conception by obtaining human semen, and themselves transferring it ...'.[25] The discussion there really deserves a detailed comparison with the Kathāvatthu, but alas, we must defer that pleasure to another time. We will consider what the other Vinayas say on this matter first, then see how the Mahāsaṅghika compares.

51 As so often in Buddhist controversies, the problem arises because of a grey area in the canonical texts, in this case the first *saṅghādisesa*. *Saṅghādisesa* is the second most serious class of offence in the Vinaya. While the most

---

[24] Kathāvatthu 2.6.

[25] The *Malleus Maleficarum* (*The Witch's Hammer*) is a textbook published in 1486 by two Dominican monks on how to identify and subjugate witches. http://www.malleusmaleficarum.org/part_I/mm01_03a.html

serious class of offences, the *pārājikas*, entail immediate and permanent expulsion from the Sangha, *saṅghādisesa* requires a period of rehabilitation involving loss of status, confession of the offence to all bhikkhus, and similar mild but embarassing penances.

52 The basic rule for *saṅghādisesa* 1 is identical in all existing *pāṭimokkhas*: 'Intentional emission of semen, except in a dream, is a *saṅghādisesa*'. In the Pali, the background is this. First the rule was laid down simply for 'intentional emission of semen'. Then a number of bhikkhus had gone to sleep after eating delicious food, without mindfulness, and had wet dreams. They were afraid they had committed an offence. The Buddha said: 'There is intention, but it is negligible.'[26] Thus there is no offence for a wet dream, but this is a practical concession for Vinaya purposes, not an admission that there is no ethical content to wet dreams. The point is made clear in Kathāvatthu 22.6, where the Mahāvihāravāsin specifically refutes the proposition (attributed by the commentary to the Uttarapāthakas) that dream consciousness is always ethically neutral.

53 The Pali rather curiously repeats the story of the mindless, greedy monks emitting semen as a pretext for allowing the use of a sitting cloth to prevent the dwelling from being soiled.[27] Why such a cloth should be called a 'sitting cloth' (*nisīdana*) is unclear, and the use of such a small cloth rapidly proves inadequate, so the Buddha allows a sleeping cloth 'as large as you like'. This passage, which appears to spring from the same origin as the *saṅghādisesa* story, adds some emphatic messages.

54
> 'Those, Ānanda, who fall asleep with mindfulness established and clearly comprehending do not emit impurity. Even those ordinary people who are free from lust for sensual pleasures, they do not emit impurity. It is impossible, Ānanda, it cannot happen, that an arahant should emit impurity.'[28]

55 The text lists five dangers of falling asleep unmindfully: One sleeps badly, wakes badly, has nightmares, devas don't protect one, and one emits semen. Those who sleep mindfully may expect the corresponding five benefits.

---

[26] Pali Vinaya 3.112: *Atthesā, bhikkhave, cetanā; sā ca kho abbohārikāti.*

[27] Pali Vinaya 1.294.

[28] Pali Vinaya 1.294: *Ye te, Ānanda, bhikkhū upaṭṭhitassatī sampajānā niddaṁ okkamanti, tesaṁ asuci na muccati. Yepi te, Ānanda, puthujjanā kāmesu vītarāgā tesampi asuci na muccati. Aṭṭhānametaṁ, Ānanda, anavakāso yaṁ arahato asuci mucceyyāti.*

56 A list of five dangers/benefits occurs in similar contexts in the Sarvāstivāda,[29] Dharmaguptaka,[30] and Mahīśāsaka[31] Vinayas. The Sarvāstivāda moreover adds the following: 'Even if a bhikkhu who is not free of greed, hatred, and delusion sleeps with unconfused mindfulness and unified mind he will not emit semen; still more a person free from lust.'[32] The Mahīśāsaka adds a similar statement: 'If one who is not free from greed, hatred, and delusion goes to sleep with mind distracted and confused, they will emit semen; even if unable to be free, going to sleep with established mindfulness, one will not commit that fault.'[33] I have not found similar statements in other Vinayas. These are similar to the statements found in the Pali Vinaya, but I have found nowhere else that declares so emphatically that it is impossible for an arahant to emit semen in a dream.

57 The Mūlasarvāstivāda Vinaya, while preserving an identical *saṅghādisesa* rule, gives only a brief, formulaic origin story, and no statement that one emits after falling asleep mindlessly, although it does speak of having sensual desire while in the dream.[34] This suggests that nocturnal emissions are a product of defilements, but is much less explicit than the other Vinayas on this point. The whole rule is dealt with relatively briefly, but this is typical of this section of this Vinaya, so the brevity is more likely to be a literary characteristic than a sectarian difference.

58 Thus all the Vinayas preserve the same rule against emitting semen. With the exception of the Mūlasarvāstivāda, the Sthavira schools all contain strong admonitions emphasizing that wet dreams occur because one

---

29 一者無難睡苦。二者睡易覺。三者睡無惡夢。四者睡時善神來護。五者睡覺心易入善覺觀法 (T23, № 1435, p. 197, a18–20). The last is different: one easily enters wholesome thoughts.

30 1. Nightmares; 2. Not guarded by devas; 3. Mind doesn't enter thought of Dhamma; 4. One does not gain perception of light; 5. One emits semen (一者惡夢。二者諸天不護。三者心不入法。四者不思惟明相。五者於夢中失精 (T22, № 1428, p. 579, b25–27)).

31 1. Nightmares; 2. Not guarded by devas; 3. Not gain perception of light; 4. No thought of Dhamma in mind; 5. Emits semen (一者惡夢。二者善神不護。三者不得明想。四者無覺法心。五者失不淨 (T22, № 1421, p. 10, b22–24)). This is identical with the Dharmaguptaka, except items three and four are swapped.

32 比丘有婬怒癡未離欲。不亂念一心眠。尚不失精。何況離欲人 (T23, № 1435, p. 197, a20–22, also T23, № 1435, p. 197, a20–22).

33 若未離欲恚癡散亂心眠必失不淨。雖未能離。以繫念心眠者無有是過 (T22, № 1421, p. 10, b27–29).

34 夢中雖有情識 (T24, № 1458, p. 540, b28–29).

goes to sleep unmindfully. The Mahāvihāravāsin, Sarvāstivādin, and Mahīśāsaka also say that even an unenlightened person can prevent wet dreams by mindful sleeping, still more an enlightened one. The Mahāvihāravāsin alone explicitly declares that it is impossible for an arahant to emit semen.

59 In the Mahāsaṅghika Vinaya the origin story is quite different to the Mahāvihāravāsin. After the initial laying down of the rule, there were two trainees (i.e. *ariyas* but not arahants) and two ordinary people who had wet dreams. They doubted and told Sāriputta, who told the Buddha. The Buddha said:

> 60 'Dreams are unreal, not true. If dreams were real, one who practiced the holy life in my Dhamma would not find liberation. But because all dreams are untrue, therefore, Sāriputta, those who practice the holy life in my Dhamma reach the end of suffering.'[35]

61 Then it lists (and defines) five kinds of dream: true dreams (such as the dreams of the Bodhisattva before his awakening); false dreams (when one sees in a dream what is not true when awake); unrealized dreams (having woken, one does not remember); a dream inside a dream; dreams born of thinking (one plans and imagines during the day, then dreams about it at night).[36]

62 Then the text gives us five causes of erections: sensual desire; excrement; urine; wind disorder; contact with non-humans.[37] A similar list is found in the Pali cases for the first *pārājika*, in the context of affirming that an arahant can have an erection:

> 63 'There are, monks, these five causes of erections: lust, excrement, urine, wind, or insect bite. These are the five causes for an erection. It is impossible, monks, it cannot happen that that bhikkhu could have an erection out of lust. Monks, that bhikkhu is an arahant.'[38]

---

[35] 夢者虛妄不實。若夢眞實。於我法中修梵行者。無有解脫。以一切夢皆不眞實。是故舍利弗。諸修梵行者於我法中得盡苦際 (T22, № 1425, p. 263, a26–29).

[36] 者實夢。二者不實夢。三者不明了夢。四者夢中夢。五者先想而後夢 (T22, № 1425, p. 263, b8–10).

[37] 身生起有五事因緣。欲心起。大行起。小行起。風患起。若非人觸起 (T22, № 1425, p. 263, b20–21).

[38] Pali Vinaya 3.39: *Pañcahi, bhikkhave, ākārehi aṅgajātaṁ kammaniyaṁ hoti–rāgena, vaccena, passāvena, vātena, uccāliṅgapāṇakadaṭṭhena. Imehi kho, bhikkhave, pañcahākārehi aṅgajātaṁ kammaniyaṁ hoti. Aṭṭhānametaṁ, bhikkhave, anavakāso yaṁ tassa bhikkhuno rāgena aṅga-*

64 The last point is crucial: in the Pali it refers to 'bites of caterpillars and little creatures', whereas the Mahāsaṅghika speaks of 'non-humans', a term widely used of spirit beings, and so including 'conveyance by Māra'.

65 So the Mahāsaṅghika does not contain any statement condemning wet dreams, or attributing them to mindlessness. While the Mūlasarvāstivāda is also silent on the topic, in that case it is a mere omission, whereas the Mahāsaṅghika trys to justify certain wet dreams with the curious doctrine about the unreality of dreams (which is contradicted immediately below!) Similarly, they appear to have rephrased the five causes of erections to suggest the possibility of Māra's involvement.

66 On this basis, we are justified in seeing a sectarian divergence in this Vinaya issue. All the Vinayas are concerned about wet dreams. The Sthavira schools, with the dubious exception of the Mūlasarvāstivāda, condemn them with varying degrees of stridency, while the Mahāsaṅghika are concerned to excuse them. There seems little doubt that this difference is connected with the root cause of the separation between the schools on the basis of the 'five theses'. Since this Vinaya was found in Pāṭaliputra, it should be seen as relevant to the central or mainstream Mahāsaṅghika, not just to their later sub-schools.

67 As with so many doctrinal points that are theoretically 'Theravādin', there is no unity on this question in contemporary Theravāda. The question is usually discussed out of the public arena, but has made its way into at least one contemporary publication. Some modern Theravādins hold that nocturnal emissions can be a purely natural occurrence, saying: 'When the pot's full, it overflows'. The question has sometimes arisen due to circumstances identical with those depicted in the story of Mahādeva: an attendant washes the robes of a revered monk and discovers unexpected evidence of 'outflows'. While not wishing to pass judgement on whether an arahant can have an emission, we can say that some monks who have said this in modern times are genuinely well practiced meditation masters. Whether correct or incorrect, they are nothing like the corrupt Mahādeva who lurches forth out of the feverish imagination of the Mahāvibhāṣā.

---

jātaṁ kammaniyaṁ assa. Arahaṁ so, bhikkhave, bhikkhu. The identical list in Mahīśāsaka Vinaya *saṅghādisesa* 1, except sensual desire is last (T22, № 1421, p. 10, b26–27).

5.4 Dhamma or Vinaya?

68 We have seen various causes proposed for the root schism. The two that appear to stand out are the status of the arahant and textual revision. However it is sometimes argued that the schisms must have been based on Vinaya grounds, for the Vinaya itself defines schism as performance of separate *uposathas* in the same monastic boundary. But this is suspiciously self referential: of course the Vinaya sees schism as a Vinaya matter—how else? The reality is that Dhamma and Vinaya are never separate in practice, and so the Vinayas repeatedly and explicitly emphasize that schism can be due to either Dhamma or Vinaya.

69 We are still left with our problem: what was the cause of the root schism—was it Dhamma or Vinaya? I think we have sufficiently shown that there is no basis whatsoever for concluding that Vinaya practice was the cause: none of our sources say this. But this leaves us little closer to a solution, for all such boundaries are inevitably permeable. We are dealing with a variety of subtly interrelated questions of practice, textuality, self definition, communal survival, philosophical evolution, and so on. The surviving fragments we happen to have inherited don't come with a guarantee that they are capable of yielding a 'correct' interpretation.

70 I am reminded of a memorable sequence in the documentary 'The Fog of War'. Robert McNamara, the US Secretary for Defence during the Kennedy and Johnson administrations, reminisces about a social dinner he organized in the early 90s with his opposite number during the Vietnam War (whose name I forget). As the dinner went on, the discussion became more and more heated. McNamara was trying to convey the point that the Americans were only interested in stopping the progress of communism. The Vietnamese gentleman insisted that the Americans wanted to colonize Vietnam. McNamara denied this point blank, alleging that Vietnam was the next domino that would allow Chinese communism to take over Asia. The Vietnamese representative said this was ridiculous: they had been colonized by the Chinese for over 1000 years, and Chinese domination was the last thing they wanted. As the conversation went on, it became more and more clear that the two sides had been fighting two quite different wars. The Americans were fighting for global ideological supremacy, while

the Vietnamese were fighting a war for national independence. The real problem was neither communism nor colonialism, but the inability to listen to each other.

71 In our diverse accounts of the schisms, with some sides alleging textual shenanigans, others speaking of doctrinal corruptions, and so on, surely we have a similar situation. We know that all of these things were in fact going on: everyone was revising and updating their texts, everyone was refining their doctrinal perspectives. This process is still continuing today. But only rarely does it lead to schism. The cause of the schism was neither the five theses nor the textual revisions, but the inability to listen.

72 This can easily be compared with the modern situation. There are many Buddhists around with many different views, far more divergent than in the early period in India. Some of these Buddhists are interested in dialogue and engagement with Buddhists of other traditions, and are quite open to learn from them. Some, on the other hand, are content with their own tradition, ignoring or even openly condemning other Buddhist traditions. Within both of these groups, however, there are a diversity of views and doctrines. Theravādins don't stop being Theravādins because they talk with Tibetans. Zen practitioners don't take up tantra just because they see a sand mandala. Views do change, mutual conditioning does happen, but the result is an infinite variety of perspectives and approaches, not a homogenous blend. The key difference is not that one group has clearly distinct doctrines and the other doesn't, but that one group is interested in dialogue and the other isn't.

73 This is why the real difference in the accounts of the schisms does not lie in the factual details that we have so laboriously tried to unravel, but the difference in emotional tones. The Sarvāstivādin, Mahāvihāravāsin, and Puggalavāda treatises demonize (literally!) their opponents. The Śāriputraparipṛcchā, on the other hand, stands out for its gentle acceptance of the schism. While it naturally favours its own school, this does not lessen its appreciation of other schools.

Chapter 6

MORE ON THE VIBHAJJAVĀDINS

OUR UNDERSTANDING OF THE TERM *VIBHAJJAVĀDA* has been put on a sounder footing by L. S. Cousins in his paper 'On the Vibhajjavādins'. He treats the term as twofold, signifying both the teachings of the Buddha in general, and also the name of a specific Buddhist school, or set of closely related schools. The basic position would seem to be that the Vibhajjavādins emerged as one of the major early schools. The first division was between the Sthaviras and Mahāsaṅghikas. Then the disputes on the 'person' and 'all exists' produced respectively the Puggalavāda and Sarvāstivāda schools (or groups of schools, or philosophical movements). What remains is the Vibhajjavāda, which, due mainly to geographical separation, gradually differentiated into the Mahāvihāravāsins,[1] Dharmaguptakas, Mahīśāsakas, and Kaśyapīyas, and perhaps others.

2 There is no doubt that certain sources, such as Bhavya II and III, clearly present such a group of Vibhajjavādin schools. It is less clear that this

[1] Cousins uses the term Tambapaṇṇiya ('Those from the Isle of Tambapaṇṇa') to refer to the Sinhalese school that today we call 'Theravāda'. I prefer to use Mahāvihāravāsin, as it more clearly differentiates the 'Theravādins' from the later Sinhalese schools, who might equally be called 'Tambapaṇṇiya'. The views accepted as 'Theravādin' are those authorized by the Elders of the Mahāvihāra; the large number of dissenting voices recorded in the commentaries show that the 'orthodox' views were at no time accepted *in toto* by all the monks of Sri Lanka.

situation is relevant in the early period. And it is not clear at all that such a group was ever imagined by the Sinhalese. So we need to inquire into the use of the word in our Sinhalese commentarial accounts of the Aśokan period.

3 Cousins acknowledges that one of our earliest sources for the term is in the commentary to the Kathāvatthu.[2] This is a version of the Third Council, where the good monks and Moggaliputtatissa reassure king Aśoka that the Buddha was a *vibhajjavādin*. There, the context suggests of the kind of ambiguity Cousins sees in the term:

> 4 'The whole point of the story is that no-one can deny that the Buddha was a *vibhajjavādin*, since he is at least sometimes so portrayed in the canonical texts. Nor of course is it surprising if a leading figure of the *Vibhajjavādin* school asserts that he was a *Vibhajjavādin*. None of this gives us any reason to suppose that the Buddha would have been referred to in the third person as a *vibhajjavādin* prior to the adoption of the word as the name of a school.'[3]

5 Actually, Cousins' prose is itself ambiguous: the 'leading figure of the *Vibhajjavādin* school' (i.e. Moggaliputtatissa) used the term *vibhajjavādin* to refer to the Buddha, not to himself. The text does not preclude the possibility that the Buddha was referred to as a *vibhajjavādin* before the formation of a school of that name. In fact, I would say that the main thrust of the passage means just that. Indeed, the Buddha is referred to in the third person as a *vibhajjavādin* in the canonical text that Cousins has already quoted.[4]

6 What Cousins is getting at, I think, is that the canonical sources are few and fairly minor. They apply only in specific contexts and speak of how the Buddha would respond when presented with certain questions. Thus they are an insufficient basis to form a general characterization of the Buddha as *vibhajjavādin*. Cousins therefore concludes that when certain texts choose this particular term to characterize the Buddha's doctrine, this cannot be explained on the basis of the canonical texts, but must have occurred after the formation of a school called *vibhajjavāda*, which then tried to authorize itself by claiming that the Buddha was a *vibhajjavādin*.

---

[2] Kathāvatthu Aṭṭhakathā, 7; LAW, 6.

[3] COUSINS, 'On the Vibhajjavādins', 138.

[4] Aṅguttara Nikāya 10.94 at AN v.189*f*.

7 But this just defers the argument: neither here nor anywhere else does Cousins attempt to explain why, given that *vibhajjavāda* is such a marginal term in the canon, should any school choose to call itself that. We therefore propose to re-examine the sources.

6.1 The Kathāvatthu

8 The Pali account of the Third Council has Aśoka asking the good monks what the Buddha taught (*kiṁvādī bhante sammāsambuddhoti?*) to which they reply the Buddha was a *vibhajjavādin* (*vibhajjavādī mahārājāti*). Notice the same, rather ambiguous suffix *-vādī* ends both phrases. This spans a spectrum of meaning, from 'speaks', to 'teaches', to 'has a doctrine of', to 'adheres to the school teaching such a doctrine'. In this case, the king could hardly have meant: 'What school did the Buddha belong to?'[5] Nor was he asking for a detailed exposition of the many teachings give by the Buddha in his career. He needed a concise, pithy summary of the Buddha's key doctrine. The monks at the time would have been familiar with the Buddha's skill in adjusting the teachings to time, place and person, and so would have chosen a message that was directly targeted to solving the urgent problem confronting the king.

9 Here the Mahāvihāra's version of events, as recorded in the Samantapāsādikā,[6] the Kathāvatthu-aṭṭhakathā,[7] and elsewhere[8] takes another

[5] COUSINS ('On the Vibhajjavādins', 171 note 73), on the contrary, believes that this is exactly what the the 'underlying reference' to the question was. Hence he does not translate the phrase according to what he admits is the meaning in the Sutta passages: 'What does the Buddha teach?' In such remarks we see the distorting effects of reading sectarian agendas into Aśokan passages.

[6] Samantapāsādikā 1.61: *Tasmiṁ samāgame moggaliputtatissatthero parappavādaṁ maddamāno kathāvatthuppakaraṇaṁ abhāsi. Tato saṭṭhisatasahassasaṅkhyesu bhikkhūsu uccinitvā tipiṭakapariyattidharānaṁ pabhinnapaṭisambhidānaṁ tevijjādibhedānaṁ bhikkhūnaṁ.*

[7] Kathāvatthu-aṭṭhakathā 7: *Tasmiṁ samāgame moggaliputtatissatthero yāni ca tadā uppannāni vatthūni, yāni ca āyatiṁ uppajjissanti, sabbesampi tesaṁ paṭibāhanatthaṁ satthārā dinnanayavaseneva tathāgatena ṭhapitamātikaṁ vibhajanto sakavāde pañca suttasatāni paravāde pañcāti suttasahassaṁ āharitvā imaṁ parappavādamathanaṁ āyatilakkhaṇaṁ kathāvatthuppakaraṇaṁ abhāsi. Tato saṭṭhisatasahassasaṅkhyesu bhikkhū uccinitvā tipiṭakapariyattidharānaṁ pabhinnapaṭisambhidānaṁ.* Translation at LAW, 7.

[8] E.g. Dīpavaṁsa 6.40: *Maddivā nānāvādāni nīharivā alajjino / Sāsanaṁ jotayivāna kathāvathuṁ pakāsayi.* Also see Dīpavaṁsa 6.55, 56.

turn: after the settling of the dispute, the leading Elder, Moggaliputtatissa, is said to compose the Kathāvatthu, and 1000 monks are chosen to authorize the Third Council adding this work to the Tripitaka. But let us compare these passages with the parallel in the Sudassanavinayavibhāsā.[9]

Table 6.1: Moggaliputtatissa and the Kathāvatthu

Sudassanavinayavibhāsā	Samantapāsādikā	Kathāvatthu-aṭṭhakathā
In that gathering Moggaliputtatissa acting as the Elder refuted the wrong doctrines of followers of other religions. The assembly chose those knowledgable in the Tripitaka and the three-fold realization, numbering 1000 bhikkhus.	In that gathering the Elder Moggaliputtatissa, refuting other doctrines, spoke the Kathāvatthu treatise. And then from the bhikkhus reckoned as 6 000 000 were chosen bhikkhus who were memorizers of the Tripitaka, distinguished in the *paṭisambhidas*, endowed with the three-fold realization, etc., numbering 1000 bhikkhus.	In that gathering the Elder Moggaliputtatissa, regarding those issues that had arisen and those that would arise in the future, for the sake of dispelling all of them, using the method that had been given by the Teacher, the Tathāgata, arranged the matrix distinguishing 500 statements of one's own school and 500 of the other schools. Having brought together 1000 statements he spoke this Kathāvatthu treatise, of futuristic character, for the sake of refuting other doctrines. And then from the bhikkhus reckoned as 6 000 000 were chosen bhikkhus who were memorizers of the Tripitaka, distinguished in the *paṭisambhidas*, numbering 1000 bhikkhus.

10 Notice that the Samantapāsādikā adds three phrases: the mention of the Kathāvatthu, the exaggerated number (elsewhere the Sudassanavinayavibhāsā mentions 60 000), and the mention of the *paṭisambhidas.* The Kathāvatthu commentary adds further details describing the Kathāvatthu itself, which one might expect. This addition refers to the legend that the Buddha had designed the basic framework of the Kathāvatthu in order that Moggaliputtatissa should fill in the details. Interestingly, it says that the

[9] 於集眾中。目揵連子帝須爲上座。能破外道邪見徒眾。眾中選擇知三藏得三達智者一千比丘 (T24, № 1462, p. 684, b9–11).

orthodox and heterodox views should be 'divided' (*vibhajanto*); as this passage follows immediately after the passage mentioning the *vibhajjavāda*, perhaps this offers a clue as to what this means here. Notice that the Kathāvatthu-aṭṭhakathā loses the statement that the 1000 bhikkhus chosen to perform the Third Council all possessed the three realizations: thus the early Sutta and practice based ideal of an arahant is sidelined in favor of the Mahāvihāravāsin textual ideal.

11 All of these changes apparent in the Pali versions as compared with the Sudassanavinayavibhāsā are absolutely characteristic of the Mahāvihāra's perspective. I cannot see any other reasonable conclusion than that the additions to the Samantapāsādikā and Kathāvatthu-aṭṭhakathā are all interpolations at a late date in the Mahāvihāra, presumably made by Buddhaghosa. It would seem that the original version of the Third Council did not mention the Kathāvatthu.

12 The Kathāvatthu is an extensive refutation of heretical views, but of Buddhist heretical views. Thus there is a decided tension in the story: are we supposed to see this account as a purification of the Sangha from non-Buddhist heresies (eternalism, etc.), or wrong interpretations of Buddhist teachings? Perhaps we are tempted to synthesize these perspectives; after all, the first and main debate in the Kathāvatthu is against the *puggala*, the 'person', who, in a suspiciously Self-like manner, is supposed to somehow exist outside the 5 aggregates and to pass on from one life to the next. Perhaps there is something to this, as Buddhists, sometimes justifiably, often suspect 'innovations' of practice or doctrine to be 'Hindu' influences. This is perhaps suggested when the Kathāvatthu commentary ascribes the *puggala* controversy to: 'In the sasana, the Vajjiputtakas and Saṁmitiyas, and many other teachers not belonging to the sasana.'[10]

13 Yet the debate on the *puggala* primarily revolves around a tension within Buddhist doctrine. When the Buddha taught, he was surrounded by 'Self' religions, and of necessity had to emphasize 'not-self'; that is, against those who would assert the absolute unity of the person, he emphasized that what we call a 'self' is an abstraction inferred from experience, motivated by fear of death and dissolution, but which, when we look for it in experience, cannot be found. Thus, against those who asserted to abso-

[10] Kathāvatthu Aṭṭhakathā 9.

lute primacy of unity, he proposed the contemplation of diversity, without, however, reifying that diversity into another absolute.[11]

14 This is effective as a philosophical counter to self-theories, but leaves us having to seek an explanation for why we feel or experience a sense of 'identity': why, if there is no truly eternal core or essence, do we nevertheless feel as if we are a person? Certain indications in the canonical texts suggest ways of approaching this problem, but the schools were left to work out their own definitive solutions. For some schools, such as the Mahāvihāravāsins, the sense of identity was explained in terms of causal relations among disparate elements. But for the Puggalavādins this was not enough, so they attempted to 'draw out' certain Sutta passages as implying the existence of a 'person' (*puggala*) in some sense outside the five aggregates, which was, however, not the Self spoken of by the non-Buddhists. For them, this was a 'middle way' between the self-theories and the absolute 'no-self' of the Abhidhamma theorists.

15 Thus we are justified in thinking of the Puggalavāda schism as primarily an internal matter among Buddhists, and while not denying any connection with non-Buddhist teachings, would resist an attempt to simply 'collapse' the two issues we are presented with at the Third Council: the infiltration of non-Buddhist heretics, and the development of Buddhist philosophical ideas as debated in the Kathāvatthu. Our text makes no attempt at a synthesis of these perspectives, but rather leaves us with an impression of disparate, although perhaps related, agendas.

16 Given this situation, and given the flow of the text as preserved by the Mahāvihāravāsins, what role was played by the term *vibhajjavādin*? Why was this term chosen, and how was it useful at this time? How would it have served as a key to solving the king's dilemma?

6.2 Later Mahāvihāravāsin sources

17 Cousins quotes and translates passages from the later Mahāvihāravāsin literature that define what *vibhajjavāda* means to them. They say, for example, that the Buddha was a *vibhajjavādin* because he *distinguished* the

[11] Cf. SN 12.48: 'All is oneness: that is the third cosmological speculation ... All is diversity: that is the fourth cosmological speculation ...'

various senses in which he could be called 'one who leads astray' (i.e. he leads astray from unwholesome things); or he *distinguished* the kinds of pleasant feeling or the various kinds of thoughts to be cultivated or not (according to whether they conduce to wholesome states of mind).

18 But as Lamotte comments: ' ... that is a state of mind which is fitting for all Buddhist thinkers in general and it could not have served Aśoka in establishing the orthodoxy of the Aśokārāma monks and separating non-believers from the true faithful.'[12] Simply making rational distinctions is never regarded by Buddhists as a distinguishing feature of their religion, or of their particular school.

19 For example, the Mahāvibhāṣā depicts Mahādeva, who it sees as the corrupt founder of the Mahāsaṅghika school, making subtle *distinctions* between the kinds of doubt an arahant might have or not have; or the kinds of 'outflows' an arahant might have or not have, and so on. This is exactly the kinds of *distinctions* meant by the general use of *vibhajja*, and they are entirely characteristic of the *vibhajjavādins'* supposed enemies.

20 Or in non-Buddhist circles, we need only think of the Jains, whose cardinal philosophy is the *anekantavāda*, the doctrine of 'not just one standpoint'. They hold that any truth may be seen from many different perspectives, so no one perspective can be privileged as ultimate. On the contrary, as Cousins points out, the Buddha himself, while sometimes using the method of *distinguishing*, in other contexts makes *unequivocal* (*ekaṁsa*) statements. Since such unequivocal teachings include the four noble truths, it could be seriously argued that the Buddha was an *ekaṁsavādin.*[13]

21 The late Pali texts also, as shown by Cousins, use *vibhajjavāda* to distinguish the Mahāvihāravāsin school from others, claiming to be the only true *vibhajjavādins*, and specifically mentioning some doctrines of other schools. This perhaps includes the Sarvāstivāda term *hetupaccaya*, although this is unclear. More clear is the term 'undefiled ignorance', which was accepted by the Sarvāstivādins and others,[14] and 'noncommunicating materiality', which was accepted by the Vaibhāṣika Sarvāstivādins, and possibly others. But these doctrines are all advanced Abhidhamma topics, which, even if

---

[12] LAMOTTE, *History of Indian Buddhism*, 274.

[13] COUSINS, 'On the Vibhajjavādins', 134.

[14] Undefiled ignorance would also seem to relate to one of the five theses.

they were current at that early time, would have had little relevance to the king's dilemma.

22 So we conclude that the meanings of the word *vibhajjavādin* proposed by Cousins based on the Pali canon and commentaries are not adequate to account for its use in the Third Council narrative.

6.3 What does 'Vibhajjavāda' mean?

23 So we are left with the problem: what did *vibhajjavāda* mean, and why was it relevant in the context of the Third Council? Let us recall the flow of the text. The non-Buddhist heretics assert various doctrines of the 'self'; Moggaliputtatissa opposes them with the Buddha's doctrine of *vibhajjavāda*; then the Mahāvihāra sources depict him as going on to teach the Kathāvatthu. Even if the Kathāvatthu was a later addition, the Mahāvihāra must have added it for some reason. The Kathāvatthu commentary, as we have seen, specifically says that the Kathāvatthu 'distinguishes' (*vibhajanto*) the heterodox and orthodox views, so perhaps it means to make some explicit connection between the Kathāvatthu and the *vibhajjavāda*.

24 Now, the Kathāvatthu discusses very many topics, many of which are trivial and are given little space, and far outweighing all other topics in the book is the first section, the discussion of the 'person'. This is, as we have seen, the only main topic common to the Kathāvatthu and the Vijñānakāya, apart from the opposing positions on the 'all exists' thesis. It was clearly a difficult controversy, and despite the cool Abhidhamma dialectic, an emotional one.

25 In our present context, surely the emerging theme is this self/not-self debate. I would like to suggest that the term *vibhajjavāda* is used here to imply a critique of the non-Buddhist theory of Self. This would certainly fulfil the criteria we asked for earlier, that the term must evoke a pithy, essential aspect of the Buddha's teaching in a way that would answer the challenge of the heretics.

26 The teaching of not-self has always been regarded as a central doctrine of the Buddha. A characteristic method used by the Buddhists to break down the false idea of self was to use *analysis*. In early Buddhism, the main method was to systematically determine those things which are taken

to be the self, hold them up for investigation, and find on scrutiny that they do not possess those features which we ascribe to a self. Thus the five aggregates are described as forming the basis for self theories. But on reflection, they are seen to lead to affliction, which is not how a self is conceived, so they fail to fulfil the criteria of a self. In the Suttas, this method was exemplified by the disciple Kaccāyana, who was known as the foremost of those able to *analyse* (*vibhajjati*) in detail what the Buddha taught in brief; the Dīpavaṁsa says that he filled that role in the First Council.[15]

27 This analysis, or *vibhaṅga*, gathered momentum during the period of the Third Council. Indeed, the basic text is called, in the Mahāvihāravāsin version, the Vibhaṅga; the Sarvāstivāda version is the Dharmaskandha, and the Dharmaguptaka version is the Śāripūtrābhidharmaśāstra. These all stem from an ancient phase of Abhidhamma development, collecting the 'analytical' Suttas, primarily arranged according to the topics of the Saṁyutta Nikāya/Āgama, and elaborating them with varying degrees of Abhidhammic exegesis.

28 So it would make perfect sense in our narrative for *vibhajjavāda* to represent the Abhidhamma movement as an analytic approach to Dhamma in general, and as a critique of the 'self' in particular. It would also seem appropriate to describe the Buddha as a *vibhajjavādin*, equivalent to saying he was an *anattavādin*. This interpretation must remain tentative, since it cannot be backed up with a clear statement from the texts. Yet, as we have seen, the definitions of *vibhajjavāda* that we are offered by the texts are inadequate to explain the usage by the Mahāvihāravāsins in their own texts: they are late, or irrelevant, or derived from a different school. If our speculations have any value, it would seem that the prime target of the polemics in this passage are not the Sarvāstivādins, but the non-Buddhist Self theorists, and perhaps by implication the Puggalavādins.

29 But there is another, quite different, aspect of the term *vibhajjavāda* that is suggested by our sources. When the troubles in the Sangha proved intractable, king Aśoka asks his ministers who can resolve the problems. They suggest Moggaliputtatissa, and so the king orders that he be fetched on a boat. Aśoka dreams that a white elephant will arrive and take him by

[15] Dīpavaṁsa 4.9.

the hand; accordingly, the next morning Moggaliputtatissa arrives, and, wading in the water to help him, the king and the Elder clasp each others' hand. This is a serious breach of royal taboos, and the guards draw their swords threateningly before being restrained by the king.

30 All this acts as a significant mythic precursor to the Third Council. With the exception of the king's dream, these events closely mirror events surrounding Upagupta; Moggaliputtatissa and Upagupta share such a close mythos that several scholars have seriously argued that they are the same monk. The only significant difference between the two in this instance is the dream sequence, which echoes the dream of the Buddha's mother before she was born, suggesting that Moggaliputtatissa, like Upagupta, is a 'second Buddha'.[16] The white elephant is also one of the seven 'treasures' of a Wheel-turning Monarch.

31 But next is another episode, which as far as I can see has no parallel with Upagupta. The king asks to see a miracle of psychic power: he wants Moggaliputtatissa to make the earth quake. The Elder asks whether he wants to see the whole earth shake, or only a part of it, saying it is more difficult to make only part shake, just as it is more difficult to make only half a bowl of water tremble. Accordingly, the king asks to see a partial earthquake, and on the Elder's suggestion, he places at a league's distance in the four directions a chariot, a horse, a man, and a bowl of water respectively, each half in and half outside the boundary. The Elder, using fourth jhana as a basis, determines that all the earth within a league should tremble: accordingly it does so, with such precision that the inside wheel of the chariot trembles, but not that outside the boundary, and the same for the horse, the man, and even the bowl of water. It was this miracle that convinced Aśoka that Moggaliputtatissa was the right man to stabilize the *sāsana*.[17]

32 The crucial value here is the precision with which the Elder can resolve his psychic abilities, dividing the earth as if with a razor. This concern for precision, orderliness, and clean boundaries is characteristic of the Mahāvihāravāsin school, which evinces a philosophical revulsion for grey areas, graduations, and ambiguities.

---

[16] Sudassanavinayavibhāsā (T24, № 1462, p. 683, b21–c18).

[17] Sudassanavinayavibhāsā (T24, № 1462, p. 683, c22–p. 684, a10). This follows the Pali on every detail, except the distance is 4 *yojanas*. But 1 *yojana* at T53, № 2121, p. 179, a24.

33 For example, while other schools asserted that rebirth took place through a gradual transitional phase called the 'in-between existence', the Mahāvihāravāsins would have none of that, declaring that one life ends and the next begins in the following moment. Or while many schools spoke of a gradual penetration to the Dhamma (*anupubbābhisamaya*), the Mahāvihāravāsins developed the idea that penetration happens all-at-once (*ekābhisamaya*). Similarly, when explaining the 'Twin Miracle' where the Buddha was supposed to simultaneously emit both water and fire: the point of the miracle would seem to be the fusion of opposites, but for the Mahāvihāravāsins there is no fusion, the miracle is an example of how fast the Buddha could advert between a water-*kasiṇa* and fire-*kasiṇa*, flashing back and forth to create the illusion of simultaneity.

34 This notion of a momentary flickering back and forth to explain what the text would appear to present as synthesis is found elsewhere, too. In satipatthana the meditator first contemplates 'internally' then 'externally', then 'internally/externally'. While the Suttas regard this 'internal/external' contemplation as the comprehension that there is no fundamental difference between the two, the Mahāvihāravāsins explained it as a rapid flicking back and forth. Similarly, the Suttas speak of 'samatha and vipassana yoked together', evidently imagining a concurrent balance of these qualities in a meditator's consciousness. While the Mahāyāna sources seem to retain this understanding, the Mahāvihāravāsins again speak of a rapid alteration between the two.

35 This admittedly ill defined sense of 'clear-cut-ness' that we see in the Mahāvihāravāsins may also be implied in the usage of *vibhajjavādin*.

36 There is one final implication in the word *vibhajjavādin* in this account. One of the most dramatic episodes concerns Aśoka's initial attempt to heal the problems in the Sangha. He instructs a minister to go and order the monks to do *uposatha*. The minister is told by the good monks that they refuse to do *uposatha* with the heretics. The minister, misunderstanding Aśoka's intention, starts beheading the obstinate monks. He only stops when it he realizes that the next monk in line to have his head chopped off is none other that Tissa, the king's brother. He returns to inform Aśoka, who is understandably seized by remorse, rushes to apologize to the monks, and asks whether he is to be held karmically responsible. The monks tell

him different stories: some say he is to blame, some say he and the minister share the blame, while some say that only acts done intentionally reap a karmic result—as he had no intention there is no blame.

37 But none of them can assuage his doubt. Only Moggaliputtatissa can do this. The Elder is then sent for, and after his arrival in the boat and subsequent demonstration of his psychic powers, the king is able to accept his explanation: there is no intention, therefore there is no guilt. This episode reminds us of the spectacular State visit by Ajātasattu to the Buddha, where he similarly confessed to a great crime and was comforted by the Buddha. In both cases the king was unable to find peace of mind until hearing the Dhamma from the right person.

38 In this careful *analysis* of the distinction between physical and mental acts we see another possible meaning of *vibhajjavādin*. This was a crucial doctrine that marked off the Buddhists from otherwise similar groups such as the Jains. We have seen that Mahādeva similarly invokes such a distinction to justify his acts.

39 Thus *vibhajjavāda* might have a variety of meanings in this context. Perhaps we should not seek for a definitive answer. As a mythic text, the passage is evoking a style, an atmosphere for the school, not laying down definitions. It may be that we can go no further than to explore various possibilities. After all, the school itself did not try to close off the specific denotation of the word. But the important conclusion of this discussion is that we can find plenty of implications in the term *vibhajjavāda*, whether those explicitly offered by the tradition, or those speculatively inferred from context, that do not involve sectarian differences. This stands in marked contrast to the often assumed conception of *vibhajjavāda* as the opposite of *sarvāstivāda*, which we examine next.

Chapter 7

VIBHAJJAVĀDA VS. SARVĀSTIVĀDA?

IN NON-PALI SOURCES, *VIBHAJJAVĀDIN* is sometimes contrasted with *sarvāstivādin*. Cousins makes it clear that he sees Sarvāstivāda as distinct from *vibhajjavāda*, but does not explain why.[1] It is problematic to assume that the Mahāvihāra tradition meant to imply this contrast, since it is not found in the Pali sources.

2 Indeed, Cousins' article occasionally hints at the problems when he argues that the Vibhajjavādin schools in the narrow sense (Kaśyapīyas, Mahāvihāravāsins, Dharmaguptakas, Mahīśāsakas, Haimavatas) were a group distinct from the Sarvāstivāda. For example, he remarks that the Abhidhamma-piṭaka of the Pali school is distinct, but 'no doubt closely related to the Abhidhamma literature of other Vibhajjavādin schools'.[2] This is true, but slightly obscures the situation. Frauwallner has shown decisively that the Pali Abhidhamma Vibhaṅga is very closely related to the Sarvāstivādin Dharmaskandha. Both of these are also connected with the Dharmaguptaka's Śāriputrābhidharma, but it seems, somewhat more distantly, in form, if not doctrine. So yes, the Vibhajjavādins probably had closely related Abhidhammas, but so did the Sarvāstivādins (with the exception of the Jñānaprasthāna).

---

1 COUSINS, 'On the Vibhajjavādins', 132.
2 COUSINS, 'On the Vibhajjavādins', 166.

3 Similarly, Cousins argues that the epigraphic evidence supports the idea that the Vibhajjavādins were the main missionary schools. But of course the Sarvāstivādins are well attested in the Northwest, and the lack of inscriptions to the south merely confirms the mission account that the Sarvāstivādin patriarch Majjhantika went to Kaśmīr.

4 Classic and influential contexts for the view that *vibhajjavāda* is specifically meant to contrast with *sarvāstivāda* include Vasubandhu's Abhidharmakośa,[3] and part of the explanation for the sectarian list of Bhavya I. We should remember that this explanation is expanding on the basic list of schools in Bhavya I; but in that list *vibhajjavāda* is a synonym of *sarvāstivāda*. Such inconsistency within a single section of a text should warn us against expecting consistency across the vast schools, lands, and times of ancient Buddhism. Here is a passage from Bhavya:

> 5 'Those who say that all exists—the past, the future, and the present—are called "They who say that all exists" or Sarvāstivādins.
>
> 6 'Those who say that some things exist, (such as) past actions of which the result has not matured, and that some do not exist, (such as) those deeds of which the consequences have occurred and the things of the future; making categories (or divisions), they are called in consequence "They who speak of divisions" or *Vibhajjavādins*.'[4]

7 This view is discussed in the Kathāvatthu itself, where the opponent says that some of the past and future exists and some does not.[5] The commentary ascribes the heretical view to the Kassapīyas, who are one of the *vibhajjavādin* schools (although the Mahāvihāravāsins said they were descended from the Sarvāstivādins). Vasumitra agrees in ascribing such a view to the Kaśyapīyas.[6] In any case, the view in question is refuted by the Mahāvihāravāsins, in the book which was supposed by them to be written by Moggaliputtatissa at the very same Third Council we are considering.

---

3 若自謂是說一切有宗決定應許實有去來世。以說三世皆定實有故。許是說一切有宗。謂若有人說三世實有。方許彼是說一切有宗。若人唯說有現在世及過去世未與果業。說無未來及過去世已與果業。彼可許爲分別說部
(T29, № 1558, p. 104, b22–27).

4 ROCKHILL, 184.

5 Kathāvatthu, 151.

6 其飲光部本宗同義。謂若法已斷已遍知則無。未斷未遍知則有。若業果已熟則無。業果未熟則有 (T49, № 2031, p. 17, a27–29).

8 It is unsurprising that the northern texts would have used the term *vibhajjavādin* in a way that was actually followed by a school in the North, rather than the remote Sinhalese. But there is no particular reason to think that these passages refer to a clearly defined school; such a view may well have been held by different groups or individuals. Rather, the northern sources use *vibhajjavāda* in the sense of a doctrine specifically opposed to the *sarvāstivāda* doctrine. The Mahāvihāravāsin sources never use the term in that way, nor do they hold the view that is ascribed to the *vibhajjavādins* in those contexts.

9 This is not the only case where the northern sources attribute views to the *vibhajjavādins* that differ from the Mahāvihāravāsin perspective. The Vibhāṣā discusses the view that time is eternal, while conditioned dhammas are not eternal; conditioned dhammas migrate like fruits being taken out of one basket and placed in another.[7] This view is attributed to the Dārṣṭāntikas and Vibhajjavādins, but is not a position held by the Mahāvihāravāsins.

10 Of course, there may well be other contexts where the northern sources describe *vibhajjavādin* views that are in fact held by the Mahāvihāravāsins. But we must clearly differentiate between how the term *vibhajjavādin* is used in the different sources.

11 We saw above that in describing the use of *vibhajjavādin*, the later Pali sources do speak of doctrines that are held by Sarvāstivādins, but other schools may well have held such views as well, and the Sarvāstivādins' main tenet is not mentioned. Such contexts are clearly aimed at other Buddhist schools in general and do not specifically define *vibhajjavāda* as an alternative to the Sarvāstivādin theory of existence in the three times. In other words, there is no reason to think that in using the term *vibhajjavādin*, the Mahāvihāravāsins meant to distinguish themselves from the Sarvāstivādins in particular.

7.1 The early controversies

12 This conclusion is reinforced by examining the doctrinal sources for the discussion of the Sarvāstivāda controversy. This is found in two early

[7] FRAUWALLNER, *Studies in Abhidharma Literature*, 190*ff.*

canonical Abhidhamma works, the already mentioned Kathāvatthu of the Mahāvihāravāsins, and the Vijñānakāya of the Sarvāstivādin Devaśarman.

13 The Mahāvihāravāsins say the Kathāvatthu was composed by Moggaliputtatissa at the Third Council. The work as a whole cannot have been composed at that time, for it is the outcome of a long period of elaboration, and discusses many views of schools that did not emerge until long after the time of Aśoka. In addition, we have seen that the attribution of the work to Moggaliputtatissa at the Third Council is likely to be a late Mahāvihāra modification.

14 Nevertheless, there is no reason why the core of the book should not have been started in Aśoka's time, and indeed K. R. Norman has shown that particularly the early chapters have a fair number of Magadhin grammatical forms, which are suggestive of an Aśokan provenance. In addition, the place names mentioned in the text are consistent with such an early dating.[8] So it is possible that the main arguments on the important doctrinal issues, which tend to be at the start of the book, were developed by Moggaliputtatissa and the work was elaborated later.

15 Strong supporting evidence for this comes from the Vijñānakāya. This work starts off with extensive discussions, not of hundreds of points like the Kathāvatthu, but just two: the thesis that all exists, and the thesis of the 'person'. The Sarvāstivādins agreed with the Mahāvihāravāsins that there was no 'person' in the ultimate sense, so their refutations of the views of the Puggalavādins share much in common. But on the proposition that 'all exists' they held opposing views. For the Mahāvihāravāsins this was the sixth view discussed, but the Sarvāstivādins made it number one.

16 The first chapter is titled 'Moggallāna section.'[9] This is a debate with a monk who in the title is called 目乾連 (*mu-gan-lian*), and in the body of the text is called 沙門目連 (*sha-men mu-lian = Samaṇa Moggallāna*). Given the closeness of the two discussions of the 'person', and that Moggaliputtatissa is said by texts of both schools to have discussed this view, there seems little doubt that this is the same Elder.[10]

---

[8] See BARUA.

[9] 目乾連蘊 (T26, № 1539, p. 531, c29).

[10] Cf. COUSINS, 'The "Five Points" and the Origins of the Buddhist Schools', 58.

17 The Vijñānakāya discussion is simpler than the Kathāvatthu. Each paragraph begins with Moggallāna repeating his thesis: 'The past and future are not; the present and the unconditioned exist.'[11] The straightforwardness of this view agrees with the Kathāvatthu and disagrees with the compromise position ascribed to the Vibhajjavādins by Bhavya and Vasubandhu (as discussed earlier). Moggallāna, unfortunately, does not get much of a chance to defend his thesis, but is simply countered with a barrage of arguments based on Sutta quotes. The basic form of the argument is that in order to abandon, say, greed, one must directly 'see' it with the mind. But the seeing of the greed must be distinct from the greed itself. One therefore must be 'seeing' past occasions of greed. But one can only 'see' what really exists. Hence the past exists.[12]

18 Strangely, while every paragraph repeats this phrase, after eleven repetitions there is a different thesis, with no explanation for the difference. The remaining eight paragraphs of this section return to the original thesis, again with no explanation. The aberrant thesis is 有無所心[13] which appears to be equivalent to the Pali: *atthi anārammaṇaṁ cittaṁ* (there is mind with no object). This rather cryptic phrase seems incongruous, as it appears to have nothing to do with the question of existence in the three periods of time. But in fact it clearly partakes in the basic abhidhamma debates: for example, the threes of the Dhammasaṅgaṇī *mātikā* include 'dhammas with past object, dhammas with future object, dhammas with present object ...'.

19 Related issues are discussed in several places in the Kathāvatthu, but the most relevant is the heretical assertion that: *atītārammaṇaṁ cittaṁ anārammaṇanti* (mind with past object is without object).[14] While on the face of it self contradictory, this addresses a crucial problem: if the past and the future do not exist, what are we aware of when recollecting the past or predicting the future? Given that the non-Sarvāstivādin schools denied the existence of the past and future, they must come up with another account of this. Thus this assertion, given that it appears in the middle of

---

[11] 過去未來無。現在無爲有 (T26, № 1539, p. 532, a4–5). I have punctuated to clarify the syntax. The Pali is perhaps: *atītānāgataṁ natthi; paccuppannāsaṅkhataṁ atthi.*

[12] For an excellent discussion of this argument, see BASTOW.

[13] T26, № 1539, p. 535, a8. BASTOW does not notice this variation.

[14] Kathāvatthu 410.

a debate on the three periods of time, addresses the question of what the object of consciousness is when we think of the past and the future.

20 The view in question is ascribed by the commentary to the Uttarapāthakas, an obscure group known to no other text: it seems to be used as a generic term for the northern schools (literally 'Norwegians'!), although here it must exclude the Sarvāstivādins. It may well include the Kaśyapīyas and the Dharmaguptakas, who are well attested in the Northwest. The view of the *vibhajjavādins*/Kaśyapīyas that part of the past exists would seem to be related. Remember that, if the account of the missions is to be trusted, all these schools may claim Moggaliputtatissa as a founding teacher.

21 The Vijñānakāya and the Kathāvatthu are ascribing two opposing views to Moggaliputtatissa. Given that the Kathāvatthu is vastly more developed than the Vijñānakāya—this is the 86th view it discusses—and given that only the Vijñānakāya directly attributes this view to Moggaliputtatissa (in the Pali this attribution comes in the commentaries), we might be inclined to trust the Vijñānakāya here. On the other hand, the Sarvāstivādins may have succumbed to the temptation to denigrate their opponents by ascribing to them inconsistent views, attributing to the founder of the school views that were later held by the 'Uttarapāthakas', in which case the Kathāvatthu might be more reliable. Other possibilities remain: perhaps Moggaliputtatissa argued for both views on different occasions; or perhaps he held neither. In any case, the two texts agree that Moggaliputtatissa was involved in these discussions, and the difference is in the details of how to work out a successful psychology based on the anti-Sarvāstivāda views, rather than the basic position.

22 But the most important point for our current purpose is that neither the Vijñānakāya nor the Kathāvatthu with its commentary use the term *vibhajjavādin* in discussion of this issue. For these texts, the term *vibhajjavāda* has nothing to do with the debate on the three periods of time.

7.2 What schism?

23 While it is clear that there was debate and disagreement on this issue, it is not at all clear that this had reached a sectarian split at this time. The Kathāvatthu throughout discusses doctrines only and refrains from

referring to specific individuals or schools. Only the commentary identifies various views with particular schools. Reading the Kathāvatthu itself, we couldn't say whether the discussions were between different schools or merely an ongoing debate among one community. Of course, the lack of reference to specifics of place and time is characteristic of the Pali Abhidhamma, and perhaps we should not read anything into it.

24 But a similar process is at work in the Vijñānakāya. The first debate, on 'all exists', is directed against an individual, Moggallāna. The second debate, on the 'person', is directed against a school, the Puggalavāda.[15] Again, reading straight off the surface of the text, the debate with Moggallāna was a discussion with an individual, while the second topic was a debate between schools. This would be entirely in concordance with a situation where the Puggalavāda schism had already become manifest, so that the followers of that thesis were regarded as a distinct branch of Buddhism, while the Sarvāstivāda schism was still taking shape, still a debate among people who felt they belonged to the same school.

[15] 補特伽羅論 (T26, № 1539, p. 537, b2).

Chapter 8

DHARMAGUPTA: THE GREEK MISSIONS

AS RECORDED IN THE SRI LANKAN CHRONICLES, one of the missions traveled to Aparantaka in the west of India (Gujarat). This was led by a monk called Yonaka Dhammarakkhita, a most intriguing individual.

2 While most of the monks mentioned in the Pali sources for the Third Council come to us with only a name and a few details of their missions, Yonaka Dhammarakkhita is singled out for special honor as the teacher of Aśoka's brother Tissa. It seems that Tissa's mind was already inclining towards the Dhamma. While roaming in the forest he saw the Elder seated in meditation, being fanned by a magnificent bull elephant with the branch of a sala tree. A longing to join the Sangha arose in him, and perceiving this, Dhammarakkhita rose into the air and descended at the lotus lake in the Aśokārāma monastery in Pāṭaliputta. He bathed, all the while leaving his robes hanging in mid air. Seeing this, Tissa was so inspired he asked to join the Sangha immediately, taking Dhammarakkhita as his preceptor.[1]

3 When the missions were sent out, Dhammarakkhita went to Aparantaka, where he taught the discourse on the Great Mass of Fire and made 37 000 converts, with 1000 men and 6000 women ordaining.

4 *Yonaka* is related to 'Ionia'. It is used in Indic languages for any Westerner, especially the Greeks. Alexander the Great had led his Greek army into

---

1 Pali Vinaya 1.55.

Northwest India shortly before Aśoka. He built several cities called 'Alexandria', one of which was apparently Yonaka Dhammarakkhita's home town. Although he is said to have gone to Aparantaka, in the west of India, this is a general term and elsewhere it is clear that Dhammarakkhita stayed in Greek areas.[2]

5 The second part of his name is just as interesting. The words *rakkhita* and *gupta* have exactly the same meaning: 'guarded'. Thus some scholars (Frauwallner, Przyluski), noting that that the names Dhammarakkhita and Dharmagupta could easily be interchanged, have seen a connection between this 'Dhammarakkhita' and the 'Dharmaguptaka' school: the Dharmaguptakas were a branch of the Vibhajjavāda that developed in the wake of Yonaka Dhammarakkhita's mission in the West.[3] To verify this theory we must investigate the exact forms of his name a little closer.

6 Here are the names mentioned in the Pali missions account,[4] together with the names as recorded in the Sudassanavinayavibhāsā. Fortunately the names are phonetically recorded in the Chinese translation and the reconstruction presents no serious difficulties.

---

[2] Thūpavaṁsa 20: *Yonakaraṭṭhe alasaṇḍā nagarato yonaka dhammarakkhitatthero tiṁsa bhikkhu sahassāni* (' ... from the city of Alexandria in the Yonaka country, Yonaka Dhammarakkhita and 30 000 monks [came] ...'.) This refers to his visit to the opening of the Great Stupa in Sri Lanka.

[3] The commentaries treat the two words together, e.g. Dhammapāda Aṭṭhakathā 257: *Dhammassa guttoti so dhammagutto dhammarakkhito.*

[4] The Pali sources are fairly consistent in naming this monk, but there are occasional exceptions. In the story we have just told of Dhammarakkhita converting the king's brother, the monk is referred to as 'Yonakamahādhammarakkhita'. But the Chinese here just has Dharmagupta (曇無德 T24, № 1462, p. 682, c14). Similarly, at Mahāvaṁsa 29.39 we find Yonamahādhammarakkhita. But is is worth noticing that monk's names are subject to confusing modifications. The prefix 'Mahā' is added or not, as we have seen in the case of Yonaka [Mahā] Dhammarakkhita. There are so many names beginning with 'Dhamma-' that it is normal in modern times to drop the Dhamma and just use the second element; thus Dhammarakkhita becomes 'Rakkhita'. It is also common to name a monk by his country of origin, but again this may be applied quite inconsistently. So, without trying to sort out anything definitive, I wonder whether some of these monks might have been the same person, known by slightly different titles in different lands.

Table 8.1: Monks Named in the Aśokan Missions

Country	Pali sources	Sudassanavinayavibhāsā[1]
Kaśmīr-Gandhāra	Majjhantika	末闡提 (Majjhantika)
Mahiṁsaka-maṇḍala	Mahādeva	摩呵提婆 (Mahādeva)
Vanavāsa	Rakkhita	勒棄多 (Rakkhita)
Aparantaka	Yonaka Dhammarakkhita	曇無德 (Dharmagupta)
Mahāraṭṭha	Mahādhammarakkhita	摩訶曇無 (Mahādharmagupta)
Yonakaloka	Mahārakkhita	摩呵勒棄多 (Mahārakkhita)
Himavata	Majjhima	末示摩 (Majjhima)
	Kassapagotta	迦葉 (Kassapa)
	Alakadeva	提婆 (Deva)
	Dundubhissara	純毘帝須 (Dundubhissara)
	Sahadeva	提婆 ('another' Deva)
Suvaṇṇabhūmi	Soṇaka	須那迦 (Soṇaka)
	Uttara	鬱多羅 (Uttara)
Tambapaṇṇidīpa	Mahinda	摩哂陀 (Mahinda)
	Iṭṭhiya	地臾 (Iṭṭhiya)[2]
	Uttiya	鬱帝夜 (Uttiya)
	Sambala	參婆樓 (Sambala)
	Bhaddasāla	拔陀 (Bhadda)

[1] T24, № 1462, p. 684, c17-p. 685, a4. Hemavata teachers at T24, № 1462, p. 686, a5-9.
[2] Not found in the first section, but below at T24, № 1462, p. 684, b26.

7 Whereas the Pali has four different 'Rakkhitas', the Chinese version has two 'Rakkhitas' and two 'Dharmaguptas'. Sanghabhadra, the Chinese translator, was obviously capable of phonetically differentiating *rakkhita* from *gupta*, and we can only conclude that his manuscript contained these forms.[5] On other grounds, we are justified in regarding the Chinese version

[5] This point is unfortunately obscured in Bapat's translation, where he renders 曇無德 (*tan-wu-de*) as if it harked back to an original *dhamma[rakkhi]ta* (e.g. BAPAT, 36). But 曇無德 is the standard rendering of Dharmagupta, used dozens of times in this sense. Since we know that Sanghabhadra was quite capable of phonetically representing

of this text as being historically more reliable than the Pali,[6] so we conclude that Dharmagupta was the original form. So according to this account, two of the missionaries,[7] including the monk known in Pali as Yonaka Dhammarakkhita, were called Dharmagupta.

8 This finding from the Chinese adds considerable plausibility to the suggestion that Yonaka Dhammarakkhita was the founder of the Dharmaguptakas. Another finding not available to Przyluski and Frauwallner is the recent confirmation of extensive Dharmaguptaka presence in Greek-influenced Gandhāra.[8] This adds further strong support to the notion that the Dharmaguptakas were centered in the very same region that we find Yonaka Dhammarakkhita.

9 When we see an ancient account, with confirmed historical validity, saying that a monk called Dharmagupta lived in the Northwest; and a couple of centuries later there is substantial evidence of the strong presence of a school called Dharmaguptaka in the same region; and the records of that school confirm that they were named after their founding teacher; it would seem overly skeptical, if not actively perverse, to deny that these sources, disparate though they are, are speaking of the same person.

10 We might speculate why the Samantapāsādikā appears to have replaced Dhammagutta[9] with Dhammarakkhita, while the earlier form is still found

---

rakkhita by 勒棄多 (*le-qi-duo*), why would he use such a misleading combination of renderings within the same context? Bapat's interpretation entails that Sanghabhadra's renderings were arbitrarily inconsistent. Even for the identical Indic phonetic ending *-ta*, Sanghabhadra used two quite different characters: 德 (*de*) and 多 (*duo*). This only makes sense if 曇無德 renders Dharmagupta, since in this case the rendering is common usage, even if it is not internally consistent in this passage. I therefore think that it is virtually certain that Sanghabhadra's text read Dharmagupta (or equivalent) and Bapat's rendering as Dhammarakkhita stems from his assumption that the Sudassanavinayavibhāsā is a translation of the Samantapāsādikā; despite noting the very many differences between the two texts, he still tends to read the Pali text back into the Chinese.

6 For example, in each mission account, a number is given recording the conversions and ordinations made. (LAMOTTE, *History of Indian Buddhism*, 296) In the two accounts, in 12 cases the numbers agree. In the remaining cases the differences are, mentioning the Pali first: 100 000/1000; 37 000/7000; 37 000/30 000; 13 000/3000; 170 000 (or 137 000)/73 000; 10 000/1000. Thus whenever they differ, the Pali is larger than the Chinese, and this difference is always by a suspiciously artificial amount.

7 Unless the names are confused and they are to be counted as one.

8 SALOMON.

9 The Pali form of Dharmagupta.

in the Sudassanavinayavibhāsā. I suggest that Buddhaghosa removed the references to the Dharmaguptakas when he edited his new Vinaya commentary, the Samantapāsādikā. In this he may have been influenced by the Dīpavaṁsa, which evidently post-dates the Sudassanavinayavibhāsā.[10] The Dīpavaṁsa appears to have been the first text to have fused the account of the schisms with the account of the missions. Having issued a blanket condemnation of the Dhammaguttas,[11] it would suit the Dīpavaṁsa's polemical purpose to hide the implied connection between this school and the missions.

11 We might also wonder why the Sudassanavinayavibhāsā doesn't describe Dhammarakkhita/Dharmagupta as 'Greek' (*yonaka*). Perhaps modern usage might be relevant here. It is still the custom in Sri Lanka for foreign monks to be called by their country of origin, as for example 'Australian Sujata'. But there is, of course, no point in calling the local monks 'Sri Lankan Sujata'. So the use of the epithet *yonaka* must derive from a situation where Greek monks were considered foreign, as would have been the case in central India or Sri Lanka. But in a Greek region this would not be used. Perhaps, then, this passage from the Sudassanavinayavibhāsā is an insider's perspective, stemming from a tradition which regarded Dhammarakkhita/Dharmagupta as a local, that is, in the Northwest.

12 This would imply that the Sudassanavinayavibhāsā has a close connection with the Dharmaguptaka school. And indeed, Bapat lists many Dharmaguptaka features in the Sudassanavinayavibhāsā that were discovered by Hirakawa. For example the text mentions 24 *sekhiya* rules dealing with the stupa, an outstanding feature of the Dharmaguptaka Vinaya.[12] Where was this Dharmaguptaka flavor mixed into the text? Bapat sees this as stemming from the Dharmaguptaka influence in China when the text was translated. This interpretation is problematic, as it would imply that the translator made wholesale revisions to his text to accord with his sectarian viewpoint, whereas to my knowledge the Chinese translators did not, as a rule, make such extensive changes. The need for this interpreta-

[10] Both quote verses from the Dīpavaṁsa, but while the Samantapāsādikā names the Dīpavaṁsa, the Sudassanavinayavibhāsā says the verses were spoken by the ancients: 今說往昔偈讚 (T24, № 1462, p. 687, c3, c17–18).

[11] Dīpavaṁsa 4.36.

[12] BAPAT l–liii; see GURUGE, 96.

tion stems from Bapat's assumption that the text is a translation of the Samantapāsādikā. If we accept Guruge's argument that this text is *not* a translation of the Samantapāsādikā, but stems from an earlier Sinhalese commentary, or from a commentary used by the Abhayagiri fraternity, then it would seem more likely that the Dharmaguptaka influences were present in the original text.

13 Only the Mahāvihāravāsins and the Dharmaguptakas claim that the Brahmajāla was the first Sutta recited at the First Council.[13] I believe they placed this Sutta in this position as a mythic prototype for the Third Council, where the heretics who expound the 62 views of the Brahmajāla are expelled by Aśoka under Moggaliputtatissa's guidance. The fact that the Dharmaguptakas gave pride of place to the Brahamajāla Sutta suggests they had a similar tradition regarding the Third Council.

14 We know these affinities are there, but much more detailed work is required to ascertain exactly how or why they are there. But the conclusion seems inescapable that the Dharmaguptakas had a Vinaya commentary that included a version of the Third Council and the missions, events that are otherwise only known from the Mahāvihāravāsins.

8.1 Dharmaguptaka & 'Moggallāna'

15 The Mahāvihāravāsin tradition, together with the archaeological findings, support a connection between Dhammagutta (= Yonaka Dhammarakkhita) and Moggaliputtatissa, the leading Elder of the missions. A closer look reveals several sources linking the Dharmaguptakas and a certain 'Moggallāna'. The first of these is Vasumitra.

> 16 In this third century from the Sarvāstivādins arose another school called Mahīśāsaka. In this third century from the Mahīśāsaka arose another school called Dharmaguptaka. This school declared that Moggallāna was their main teacher. In this third century from the Sarvāstivāda arose another school called the Suvarṣaka, also called Kaśyapīya.[14]

[13] T22, № 1428, p. 968, b15–16. The Dharmaguptaka version of the Brahmajāla is very close indeed to the Pali, with only trifling variation in the sequence and wording of the 62 heretical views. For a detailed study, see CHENG.

[14] 於此第三百年中。從說一切有部。又出一部。名正地部。於此第三百年中。從正地部。又出一部。名法護部。此部自說勿伽羅是我大師。於此第三百年中。從說

17 Bhavya[15] and the San-Lun-Xian-Yi,[16] on the other hand, say that the Dharmaguptakas were so named after their founding teacher. This is natural, since the memory of Moggalliputtatissa evidently faded with time.

18 The Śāriputraparipṛcchā, in its similar account of school derivation, also connects the formation of the Dharmaguptakas with a Moggallāna. The text, which also sets itself in the third century AN, reads thus:

> 19 'The Sarvāstivādins then gave rise to the Mahīśāsakas. 目揵羅優婆提舍 (*mu-qian-luo you-po-ti-she*) started the Dharmaguptakas...'.[17]

20 Although the passage is part of the discussion of the Sarvāstivāda group of schools, the text, unlike Vasumitra, does not literally connect the Dharmaguptakas with either the Sarvāstivādins or the Mahīśāsakas, but with 目揵羅優婆提舍. The first part of this name is 'Moggalla-' or similar. The second part, 優婆提舍, usually renders *upadeśa*, in which case it would refer to a treatise by Moggallāna; remember that Moggaliputtatissa is famous for compiling the Kathāvatthu treatise. But I think it is more likely to stand for *upatissa*, which reminds us of the final part of Moggaliputtatissa's name. It is possible it refers to the early disciple Moggallāna together with his friend Sāriputta, whose personal name was Upatissa. But the Indic idiom, so far as I know, invariably pairs these two by their family names as 'Sāriputta and Moggallāna' or by their personal names as 'Upatissa and Kolita', without mixing the personal and family names.[18]

一切有部。又出一部。名善歲部。亦名飲光弟子部 (T49, № 2033, p. 20, b14–18). This is Paramārtha's translation. Xuan-zang's translation agrees, saying that the Dharmaguptakas followed the teacher Moggallāna 自稱我襲採菽氏師 (T49, № 2031, p. 15, b16–17; here Moggallāna is translated as 採菽氏, *cai-shu-shi*. This rendering derives from a story claiming that Moggallāna's family name (氏) stems from an ancestor who used to pick up (採) beans (菽, Pali *mugga*). Kumārajīva's translation says that: 'The Mahīśāsaka gave rise to another school called Dharmagupta, who followed their main teacher Moggallāna' (彌沙部中復生異部。因師主因執連名曇無德 (T49, № 2032, p. 18, b1–2). According to Li Ch'ung An there has been a carving mistake here, with 因執連 in place of 目揵連. See http://ccbs.ntu.edu.tw/FULLTEXT/JR-BJ001/03_02.htm#n36.)

[15] ROCKHILL, 184.

[16] T45, № 1852, p. 9, c13–15.

[17] 其薩婆多部。復生彌沙塞部。目揵羅優婆提舍。起曇無屈多迦部 (T24, № 1465, p. 900, c2–4).

[18] E.g. Pali Vinaya 1.42: *Addasā kho bhagavā sāriputtamoggallāne dūratova āgacchante, disvāna bhikkhū āmantesi—'ete, bhikkhave, dve sahāyakā āgacchanti, kolito upatisso ca. etaṁ me sāvakayugaṁ bhavissati aggaṁ bhaddayugan'ti.*

21 Now the question is, do these passages refer to the Buddha's disciple Mahāmoggallāna or to the Moggaliputtatissa of the Third Council? The traditional view, recently restated by Yin Shun,[19] is that these passages refer to Mahāmoggallāna. This is understandable as Moggaliputtatissa is virtually unknown in the northern sources, so a reference to 'Moggallāna' would naturally be attributed to the great disciple.

22 The forms of the names do not decide the matter. We do not see the prefix '*mahā-*', which would definitely identify the great disciple; neither is the absence of a confirmed parallel to the second part of Moggaliputtatissa's name is not decisive, for the Vijñānakāya is definitely not referring to Mahāmoggallāna and is very likely referring to Moggaliputtatissa, but it just uses the name Moggallāna.

23 We cannot decide this question with certainty. Nevertheless, I would like to advance some considerations that, in my view, make it probable that the references in Vasumitra and the Śāriputraparipṛcchā refer to the Third Council Elder.

24 Both our sources set themselves in the third century after the Buddha. The mention of Moggallāna occurs in the course of this presentation, with no hint that they are skipping back to an earlier time. It is more natural to read the passages as if they are referring to contemporary events.

25 The name in the Śāriputraparipṛcchā is, as argued above, more likely to be a variant reading of Moggaliputtatissa than Moggallāna-Upatissa.

26 There would seem to be no cogent reason for the Dharmaguptakas to claim Mahāmoggallāna as their forebear. Normally we would expect a school to claim a forebear with whom they had some special connection: for example, the Sautrantikas honor Ānanda, the teacher of the Suttas. Mahāmoggallāna is the chief in psychic powers, but I know of no hint that this was specially emphasized by the Dharmaguptakas. On the other hand, the Sri Lankan sources show a straightforward relation between Moggaliputtatissa and Dhammarakkhita (= Dharmagupta).

27 The accounts of Vasumitra and the Śāriputraparipṛcchā are closely related, and both refer to Moggallāna: why then does the Śāriputraparipṛcchā introduce 'Upatissa'? This is perfectly understandable if we think of the name as just a variant of Moggaliputtatissa.

---

[19] http://www.budd.cn/news/budren/news_budren_20030430_9.html.

28 In Vasumitra's account, the Dharmaguptakas claim 'Moggallāna' as their teacher, and it is understandable for a school to look back to one of the historical masters as their inspiration. But the Śāriputraparipṛcchā says that Moggalla (-puttatissa or -upatissa or -upadeśa) 'started' (起) the Dharmaguptaka. It is anachronistic to speak of Mahāmoggallāna as the 'creator' of a particular school. On the other hand, it would be natural for the Dharmaguptakas to regard Moggaliputtatissa as their founding teacher.

29 As we have seen, there is reason to believe that the Dharmaguptakas had a tradition of the missions and the Third Council comparable to that of the Mahāvihāra, which emphasized the role of Moggaliputtatissa as the leader of the missionary movement. Textual support for this is found in the Sudassanavinayavibhāsā. As we have seen, the account of the missions found in this text acknowledges Moggaliputtatissa's role as the instigator of the mission of 'Dharmagupta'. If a Dharmaguptaka connection for this text is established, it would also explain the prominent role that 'Yonaka Dhammarakkhita' (= Dharmagupta) plays in the narrative.

30 The 'Moggallāna' of the Vijñānakāya is said to hold the view that there is consciousness without object. It is possible that this is a Dharmaguptaka view, for Buddhaghosa ascribes this and related views to the Uttarapāthakas,[20] and the Dharmaguptakas are likely to have been included among the Uttarapāthakas. Bhavya and Vasubandhu attribute to the Vibhajjavādins (including Dharmaguptakas) the closely related doctrine that past acts that have yielded their fruit do not exist, while past acts that have already yielded their fruit still exist. Buddhaghosa and Vasumitra ascribe this view to the Kaśyapīyas, but Vasumitra says that in most doctrines the Kaśyapīyas are similar to the Dharmaguptakas.[21] More research would need to be done to see if the Dharmaguptakas actually held the view ascribed to Moggallāna in the Vijñānakāya.

31 I therefore think we have good reason to accept the thesis that the Moggallāna referred to in connection with the Dharmaguptaka is in fact the *vibhajjavādin* Elder Moggaliputtatissa rather than the great disciple Mahāmoggallāna. This would simply make a more straightforward and reasonable explanation.

---

[20] Kathāvatthu 9.3, 9.4, 9.5, 9.6.

[21] 餘義多同法藏部執 (T49, № 2031, p. 17, b2).

8.2 Dhammarakkhita: some other stories

32 The Sri Lankan chronicles record that Yonaka Dhammarakkhita and many of his followers travelled to Sri Lanka for the inaugural blessing ceremony for the Great Stupa.[22] This is not the treatment we would expect for a schismatic, but for a respected Elder of the tradition.

33 The Abhidhamma commentaries still depict Dhammarakkhita, far off though he is, as a revered Teacher. Here is the paraphrase from the Dictionary of Pali Proper Names:

> 34 **Punabbasukutumbikaputta Tissa Thera:** He was of Ceylon, and crossed over to India, where he studied under Yonaka Dhammarakkhita. On his way home by sea he felt doubtful of one word, and returned all the way, one hundred leagues, to consult his teacher. On the way from the port he mentioned the word to a householder, who was so pleased with him that he gave him a blanket and one hundred thousand. This blanket Tissa gave to his teacher, but the latter cut it up and used it as a spread, as an example to others (not to desire luxuries). Tissa had his doubts set at rest and returned to Jambukola. There, at the Vālīkāvāma, as he was sweeping the courtyard of the cetiya, other monks asked him questions in order to vex him. But he was able to answer all these, having attained the *paṭisambhidā*. VibhA. 389.

35 The connection between Dhammarakkhita and Abhidhamma is also hinted at in a quasi-Abhidhamma post-canonical text, the Milindapañha. This text, which exists in several versions, famously records (or reinvents) a dialogue between the Greek king Milinda (Menander) and the Buddhist monk Nāgasena. The Pali version introduces a certain Dhammarakkhita in a key role. Nāgasena, after his initial training, walked 'a long way' to the east to the Aśokārāma in Pāṭaliputta in order to receive teachings from 'Dhammarakkhita'. This episode is not in the Chinese translation of the Sarvāstivāda version. It is generally agreed that the Pali version has been subject to elaboration, some blatantly unhistorical.[23] One of the purposes of this modification is to reconnect the action of the text with the Buddhist heartland in the East. Thus the text mentions five rivers: in the Chinese,

[22] Thūpavaṁsa 20. The event is earlier recorded in Mahāvaṁsa 29.39: *Yonanagarā'lasandāso, yonamahādhammarakkhito; thero tiṁsa sahassāni bhikkhū ādāya āgamā.*

[23] Such as the mention of Milinda visiting the six heretical teachers who lived in the time of the Buddha.

four of these are from the Northwest of India, but in the Pali, all are in the eastern districts.[24] Since the Milindapañha is set in the Northwest, it seems likely that the Pali editors wanted to bring the action back further east, to lands they were more familiar with, and which had a long association with the Buddhist heartland.

36 It is no coincidence that this return is to 'Aśoka's monastery', the center of the action in the Third Council story, and that it is here, with Dhammarakkhita as teacher, that Nāgasena becomes an arahant. It appears that the Pali, while celebrating the spread of the Dhamma to foreign lands, still holds the old places dear, and brings its hero back into the heartland for the crucial event of his enlightenment. Thus the insertion of the Dhammarakkhita episode is probably also to make the connection with the 'Greek Dhammarakkhita'—who better to teach the teacher of the Greeks, Nāgasena? It is unlikely that the same 'Dhammarakkhita' was alive in the time of both Aśoka and Milinda, it might just be possible.[25] But given the lack of concern for historicity displayed by the Pali editors, this does not affect the identification of the two Dhammarakkhitas.

37 Thus 'Dhammarakkhita' remained a revered elder for the Mahāvihāravāsins for a long time, fondly remembered by them as a distant brother successfully bringing the Dhamma to the Greek areas. This accords with the existing manuscript and epigraphical references to the Dharmaguptakas, which are concentrated in Gandhāra, long under Greek rule.

8.3 Dharmaguptaka texts & doctrines

38 Examination of the texts and ideas of the Dharmaguptakas confirms their close relation with the Mahāvihāravāsins. First we shall see how they are depicted in the Mahāvihāravāsin sources.

39 The Mahāvihāravāsin Kathāvatthu lists hundreds of points of contention between various schools. The schools, however, are not named in the text, and to find out who held these views—or at least, who the Mahāvihāravāsins believed held these views—we must turn to the commentary. In its introduction, the commentary classes the 'Dhammaguttikas' a branch of

[24] http://www.saigon.com/~anson/ebud/milinda/ml-01.htm.
[25] See McEvilley, 378.

the Mahīśāsakas, and hence they are reckoned among the 17 'schismatic' or 'heretical' schools. But this is merely a sweeping sectarian dismissal of all different schools. In the body of the commentary there is no mention of the Dharmaguptakas. Thus the Mahāvihāravāsins knew of the Dharmaguptakas, but they knew of no dissentient views held by them.

40 Vasumitra records the main Dharmaguptaka doctrines:[26]

- The Buddha, while living, is included in the Sangha.
- Gifts offered to the Buddha are more meritorious than those offered to the Sangha.
- Gifts made to a stupa are meritorious.
- The liberation of the Buddhas and the two vehicles (*sāvaka* and *pacceka-buddha*) is the same, though the path differs.[27]
- Non-Buddhists cannot gain the five special knowledges (*abhiññā*).
- The body of an arahant is without *āsavas.*

41 The first four of these would be acceptable to Mahāvihāravāsins; the fifth would not; the last, while being too obscure to actually make much sense to anyone except an abhidhammika, would conflict with the Mahāvihāravāsin interpretation, which holds that the body of an arahant can become the object of defilements for others; but perhaps it was intended rather as a correction to the first of the Mahāsaṅghika's '5 points'.

42 In addition to these views, Vasubandhu[28] says that the Dharmaguptakas held, in agreement with the Mahāvihāravāsins and against the Sarvāstivādins, that realization of the truths happens all at once (*ekābhisamaya*).

43 It will take us too far afield to examine in detail the actual texts of the Dharmaguptaka, but a quick survey is enough to confirm their closeness with the Mahāvihāravāsin.

44 Regarding the Dharmaguptaka Vinaya, Pachow in his survey of the *pāṭimokkhas* states: 'the Dharmaguptaka follows very closely the Pali text in most cases, not merely in numbering the series but also in contents,

---

[26] See DUTT, *Buddhist Sects in India*, 172.

[27] (This is mentioned in Xuan-zang's translation only. 佛與二乘解脱雖一。而聖道異 (T49, № 2031, p. 17, a25).

[28] Abhidharmakośa vi. 27.

except the [*sekhiya*] section, in which it adds 26 prohibitory rules regarding the Stupa.'[29]

45 Regarding the Sutta literature, McQueen studied the versions of the Sāmaññaphala Sutta, and concluded that of all of them, the Mahāvihāravāsin and Dharmaguptaka were the closest and stood nearest the ancient tradition. He also says that this closeness holds good for the Mahāvihāravāsin Dīgha Nikāya in general when compared with the Dharmaguptaka Dīrgha Āgama: 'These collections are generally quite close; major disagreements are rare. Where discrepancies do occur the [Dharmaguptaka] Dīrgha is more often wrong (late), showing corruption and expansion of the text.'[30]

46 Finally, Frauwallner in his discussion of the sole surviving Dharmaguptaka Abhidharma work, the Śāriputrābhidharma, shows its deep connections with Mahāvihāravāsin Abhidhamma books including the Dhammasaṅgaṇī, Vibhaṅga, Dhātukathā, and Paṭṭhāna. He sums up by saying 'While mainly based on old transmitted material, even this is organized in a different way as compared with the other schools we have discussed [Mahāvihāravāsin and Sarvāstivāda]. It contains little in the way of innovation or doctrinal evolution.'[31] Thus, while there are several divergences in the field of Abhidhamma, there is clearly a common source. There is no reason why extant differences should not have emerged in the long period of Abhidhamma development that took place after the separation of the schools.

47 The recent manuscript finds from Gandhāra give us a new source of Dharmaguptaka texts, and a new insight into how they developed. The existing texts, which are in a very bad state of decay, date from shortly after the Common Era, that is, the beginning of the middle period of Indian Buddhism. They lack the textual uniformity we have come to expect from the Pali, and thus Salomon suggests they stem from a time when the canon was not yet fully formed. Alternatively, it could be the case that the Dharmaguptakas did not place as much premium as the Mahāvihāravāsins on textual precision. The Dīpavaṁsa ascribes the root schism to

[29] PACHOW, 39. For a challenge to the usual interpretation that Dharmaguptakas had a special affinity for stupa worship, see: http://sectsandsectarianism.santipada.org/dharmaguptakasandthestupa.

[30] MCQUEEN, 190.

[31] FRAUWALLNER, *Studies in Abhidharma Literature*, 116.

bad textuality, and the prominence of the *paṭisambhidās* in their root treatise the Paṭisambhidāmagga confirms the centrality of textual analysis for this school. Indeed, the Mahāvihāravāsins, so far as we know, are the only school to produce a complete set of commentaries on the canonical texts. Perhaps we should regard them as the textual exegesis school *par excellence*.

48 The Gandhārī texts of the Dharmaguptakas have only been partially studied. Clearly they represent a different textual tradition to that preserved in Pali or the Chinese Āgama literature, with the obvious exception that they agree closely with the existing Chinese Dharmaguptaka texts, in so far as comparisons have been made. But there are no doctrinal differences apparent. The only really new element is the introduction of several *avadāna*-type stories relating to local celebrities. Thus the Dharmaguptakas adapted their literature to their local culture, without however changing the doctrine.

49 So it seems that the split between the Mahāvihāravāsins and the Dharmaguptakas was due to neither Dhamma nor Vinaya, but mere geography. The Dharmaguptakas were a Northwestern branch of the *Vibhajjavāda*, and the Mahāvihāravāsins or Theravādins were the southern branch. While the Mahāvihāravāsins in a belligerent mood issued a purely formal denunciation of the Dharmaguptakas, the texts, doctrines, and history instead reveal a close affinity.

Chapter 9

THE MŪLASARVĀSTIVĀDINS OF MATHURA

There are two main reasons why the Mūlasarvāstivāda school is important. The first reason is that it has left a large literary heritage, which is growing since many of the Sanskrit fragments discovered recently may possibly be from this school. The second reason is that the Tibetan Sangha owes its Vinaya lineage to this school.[1] It is important, then, to understand the place of the Mūlasarvāstivādins in Buddhist history.

2 Unfortunately, this is far from clear. The name Mūlasarvāstivāda is not found in any early inscriptions, and cannot be definitely attested until the later period of Indian Buddhism. Their Vinaya is extensive, and most modern scholars have tended to see it as late. In its current form it should be assigned to the 'middle period' of Indian Buddhism—between 500–1000 years AN—and the vagueness of this ascription tells us how little we know. Nevertheless, some scholars have claimed that it shows signs of early features in some respects. This should not surprise us, as the whole has evidently been amassed over a vast period of time, and must incorporate material from greatly different eras. If we are to ascribe the earliest features, such as the *pāṭimokkha*, to the Buddha himself, and the latest additions to, say, 500 CE, we are talking of a 1000 year period of composition!

[1] Certain Japanese monastics also follow this Vinaya. See CLARKE, 'Miscellaneous Musings on Mūlasarvāstivāda Monks.'

3 The uncertainty around this school has fuelled a number of hypotheses. Frauwallner's theory is that the Mūlasarvāstivāda Vinaya was the disciplinary code of an early Buddhist community based in Mathura, which was quite independent as a monastic community from the Sarvāstivādins of Kaśmir (although of course this does not mean that they were different in terms of doctrine). Lamotte, against Frauwallner, asserts that the Mūlasarvāstivāda Vinaya was a late Kaśmīr compilation made to complete the Sarvāstivādin Vinaya.[2] Warder suggests that the Mūlasarvāstivādins were a later development of the Sarvāstivāda, whose main innovations were literary, the compilation of the large Vinaya and the Saddharmasmṛtyupasthāna Sūtra,[3] which kept the early doctrines but brought the style up to date with contemporary literary tastes.[4] Enomoto pulls the rug out from all these theories by asserting that Sarvāstivādin and Mūlasarvāstivādin are really the same. Meanwhile, Willemen, Dessein, and Cox have developed the theory that the Sautrantikas, a branch or tendency within the Sarvāstivādin group of schools, emerged in Gandhāra and Bactria around 200 CE. Although they were the earlier group, they temporarily lost ground to the Kaśmīr Vaibhāśika school due to the political influence of Kaṇiṣka. In later years the Sautrantikas became known as the Mūlasarvāstivādins and regained their earlier ascendancy.[5] I have elsewhere given my reasons for disagreeing with the theories of Enomoto and Willemen *et al.*[6] Neither Warder nor Lamotte give enough evidence to back up their theories.

4 We are left with Frauwallner's theory, which in this respect has stood the test of time. For the remainder of this chapter I am mainly concerned with drawing out the implications of this theory. However, since this particular scenario is controversial, I will also examine another possibility. If Frauwallner is wrong, and the Sarvāstivādins and Mūlasarvāstivādins are not derived from separate Vinaya communities, it would then be likely that they are related to each other in some way. Perhaps the same school maintained different textual recensions of the Vinaya while remaining unified in practical matters. In this case we should seek for the origins of

---

2 LAMOTTE, *History of Indian Buddhism*, 178.

3 T № 721, T № 722, T № 728.

4 WARDER, 393–394.

5 Charles WILLEMEN, xi–xiii.

6 SUJATO, *A History of Mindfulness*, chapter 17, note 32.

the Mūlasarvāstivāda in relation to the origins of the Sarvāstivāda. This possibility is examined at the end of this chapter.

5 But starting off with Frauwallner, the gist of his theory is this. The Mūlasarvāstivādin Vinaya includes a section telling of the Buddha's trip to Kaśmīr, prophecying the conversion by Majjhantika. However, this section has been arbitrarily inserted in the text, showing that it is a later interpolation.[7] The earlier portions point to a connection with Mathura. This argument has recently been restated by Wynne, who defends Frauwallner's thesis, and adds the suggestion that the Mathura community later moved to Kaśmīr, where they came into conflict with the Vaibhāśikas over who could claim to be the 'real' Sarvāstivādins.[8]

6 Thus Frauwallner's theory holds that the Mūlasarvāstivāda Vinaya is the disciplinary code of a Buddhist community based in Mathura. A key piece of evidence is the statement by Kumārajīva in his translation of the Mahāprajñāpāramitopadeśa:

> 7 '(The Vinaya), in brief, contains eighty sections. It is of two kinds. The first is the Vinaya of Mathura, which includes the Jātaka and Avadāna, and comprises eighty sections. The second part, the Vinaya of Kaśmīr, has excluded the Jātaka and Avadāna;[9] accepting only the essentials, it forms ten sections. There is, however, a commentary (*vibhāṣā*) in eighty sections which explains it.'[10]

8 The Mūlasarvāstivāda Vinaya is indeed extremely long, full of Avadānas and Jātaka stories, and has strong links with Mathura. The Sarvāstivāda Vinaya, closely associated with Kaśmīr, is known as the 'Ten Part Vinaya', and does not contain the legendary and narrative material. We are, then, justified in equating these two Vinayas with the Vinayas mentioned by Kumārajīva. Frauwallner notes significant differences between these two Vinayas, and would regard the Sarvāstivāda Vinaya as in many respects closer to the other missionary schools, and probably springing from that source, while the Mūlasarvāstivāda Vinaya is an independent early lineage. While not wishing to contest this, I have noticed that on occasion

---

[7] FRAUWALLNER, *The Earliest Vinaya and the Beginnings of Buddhist Literature*, 28–36.

[8] WYNNE, 29*ff.*

[9] Stories concerning deeds done in past lives and their fruits in the present.

[10] T25, № 1509, p. 756, c2–6.

these two Vinayas do share specific features in common that suggest some connection.

9 Several sources make a further connection between the Vinaya and Upagupta, the great teacher of Mathura.[11] As the last of the five 'Masters of the Law' who were accepted throughout the northern traditions, it is natural that Upagupta's name shuld be connected with the Vinaya. And we notice that one of the most persistent attributes of Upagupta is as a preacher of *avadānas*. Indeed, so close is this connection that Strong has spoken of Upagupta as the patron of a class of monks who developed and preserved this literature. It can hardly be a coincidence, then, that of all the Vinayas known to us, the only one that features the *avadānas* so strongly hails from the home town of the great Elder so closely associated with this class of literature.

9.1 Mathura in the Suttas

10 Mathura did not have an auspicious start as a Buddhist center. The Anguttara Nikāya has the Buddha tersely remarking that in Mathura the roads are uneven, it is dusty, the dogs are fierce, the *yakkhas* are predatory, and alms-food is hard to get.[12] The background for this event is given briefly in the Pali commentary, which says that when the Buddha visited Mathura, he was greeted by a naked *yakkhinī*, who tried to either terrify or seduce him (or more likely both), out of fear he would convert all her devotees.[13] This episode is drawn out in full detail in the Mūlasarvāstivādin Vinaya, both in the Gilgit manuscripts[14] and the Chinese, and appears to have become the source of a Mūlasarvāstivādin apologetic for Mathura, which I will briefly summarize.

11 The Buddha visited Mathura and was greeted by the Brahman householders, although they were initially suspicious because it was said he did not properly respect Brahmans. Nevertheless, he taught Nīlabhūti a lesson on the caste system and they were all converted. That day was a

[11] LAMOTTE, *History of Indian Buddhism*, 175–176.

[12] Aṅguttara Nikāya 5.220.

[13] Aṅguttara Aṭṭhakathā 2.646.

[14] Gilgit Mss. 3, pt. 1:14–15.

festival day, and the Buddha was then challenged by the *yakkhinī*. It was after this episode that he spoke of the five disadvantages, similar to above. Then he told the monks not to stay at Mathura, and left to stay at the Donkey-Monster Forest. (The Pali tradition also knows a Gardabha *yakkha*: he was the doorkeeper of the famous *yakkha* Ālavaka, a childeating monster tamed by the Buddha.) The brahmans of Mathura are anxious to feed the monks and secure their blessings, for they have been plagued by child eating[15] *yakkhas* called Śara,[16] Vana,[17] and the *yakkhinī* Hārīka (訶梨迦).[18] The Indic forms of the first two of these names equate with names found in the parallel passage in the Gilgit Mss as given by Strong.[19] The final name is not equivalent to any of the names in the Gilgit Mss, but would seem very likely to be none other than the famous Hārītī, originally a goddess of smallpox in Rajagaha, who went on to have a glorious career in Buddhist popular culture, and indeed even thrives today in far off Japan. The ogres come and sit in while the Buddha is teaching Dhamma, evidently intending to spoil the event, but the Buddha admonishes them and they are converted. The townsfolk built 2500 monasteries, one for each of the 2500 *yakkhas* who have been converted.

12 We have noticed above that a certain goddess called Kuntī evidently has a family connection with Kotiputa, an early monk's name recorded at Vedisa. While the missions legend depicts Kuntī as a sweet woodlands nymph, elsewhere she takes on a more terrifying mien. The Mūlasarvāstivāda Vinaya shows her aspect as a vicious ogress who devours children.[20]

13 Other names recorded at Vedisa include Hāritīputa and Ālābagira. It now appears that all of these names are connected with child eating *yakkhas*: Hārītī, Kuntī, and Ālavaka. There are more than a few links between the stories of Hārītī and Kuntī: they are in fact the same story with a few details changed to add local color. The monasteries were named after the local *yakkhas*, implying an ongoing fusion between local deity cults and the establishment of Buddhist monasteries. It is likely that the monasteries

---

[15] 我等所生孩子。皆被侵奪 (T24, № 1448, p. 43, c2).
[16] 池 *chi*, pond.
[17] 林 *lin*, forest.
[18] T24, № 1448, p. 42, c7–p. 43, c18.
[19] STRONG, *The Legend and Cult of Upagupta*, 6.
[20] STRONG, *The Legend and Cult of Upagupta*, 34–37.

kept a shrine for the local deities that the villagers used for their traditional spirit worship cult. The villagers, it seems, would offer their children to the monastery for a period of time, perhaps in substitute for a more primitive cult of child sacrifice.

14 Our next source, from the Pali canon, is set at a monastery called the Gundāvana, the 'Gundā Grove'.[21] Soon after the Parinibbana, the disciple Mahākaccāna taught the Madhura Sutta (MN 84/SA 548) to King Avantiputta while staying at the Gundāvana. This discourse is a major statement on the invalidity of the caste system, and as such ties in neatly with the teaching to the Mathuran brahmans as depicted in the Mūlasarvāstivāda Vinaya. Such early royal patronage would have formed a strong foundation for the later growth of the Dhamma there.

15 A century later, several of the accounts of the Second Council also mention Mathura (Mahīśāsaka, Sarvāstivāda, Mahāsaṅghika, though not Mūlasarvāstivāda). One of the Elders at that Council is Śāṇavāsin, the preceptor of Upagupta, both of who are local saints of Mathura. Mathura, then, would have had a continuous occupation of Buddhist monks from the Buddha's lifetime or shortly after.

9.2 Mathura & schism

16 The community at Mathura could thus rightly regard themselves as an original community. Nevertheless, they were far enough from the main early center around Pāṭaliputta to remain a little distant from the controversies. While they were involved in the Second Council, this was the last time Buddhist monks from all districts gathered as one. There is no evidence that the Mathuran community took part in later Councils. It is true that their Elder Upagupta is frequently said to have taught Aśoka, and might therefore have participated in the various discussions that occurred at that time. But this is far from certain, and in any case, he would have done this as a visiting Elder, and this would not have directly affected the Mathuran Sangha. None of the accounts of schisms and discussions

[21] Although *yakkhas* are not mentioned, the similarity between this name (v.l. Kundavana) and Kuntī/Konta, etc., is noteworthy, given the connections between these stories.

after the Second Council mention Mathura.[22] The 'Unity Edicts' follow the southern route well away from Mathura.

17 So it seems that the Mathuran community—perhaps like many others—did not participate directly in the early schismatic movements. They developed their own scriptures, inspired by Upagupta's style, and it seems plausible that some of the early Sarvāstivāda Abhidharma ideas may have emerged here, though this is purely speculative. They are not referred to in the Mahāvihāravāsin account of the Third Council, not because they were in any sense heretical, but simply because they were an already established community who did not need missionizing.

18 In the early years there would, of course, be no need for this community to call itself by any sectarian name, since it was just another branch of the Buddhist Sangha. By the first century CE the name Sarvāstivāda appears in the Mathura region. Much later the term Mūlasarvāstivāda came into use, perhaps when the Mathura community came into competition with the Vaibhāṣika Sarvāstivādins of Kaśmir and wished to assert their primacy. There is no indication that Moggaliputtatissa used the term *vibhajjavādin* to exclude the Mathuran community that later became known as the Mūlasarvāstivādins.

19 In fact the opposite is true. We have noticed that the Mathuran Elder Śāṇavāsin lived on the Ahogaṅga/Urumuṇḍa mountain, some way out of the town.[23] Before the Third Council, Moggaliputtatissa saw the troubles brewing in the capital of Pāṭaliputta, and so went to practice at the same Ahogaṅga/Urumuṇḍa mountain monastery founded by Śāṇavāsin, which was renowned as the foremost of all places for samatha meditation. Moggaliputtatissa stayed on retreat there for seven years before reluctantly descending on the invitation of Aśoka to resolve the problems at the Third Council.[24] Thus the Mathuran community, in the lineage of Śāṇavāsin, far from being schismatic, is the place Moggaliputtatissa would go on retreat to escape from the schismatic problems.

[22] I have earlier suggested that the Śāriputraparipṛcchā could have originated in a dispute in Mathura; but if this tentative hypothesis is true, it refers to a later period.

[23] Pali Vinaya 2.298: *Tena kho pana samayena āyasmā sambhūto sāṇavāsī ahogaṅge pabbate paṭivasati.*

[24] Samantapāsādikā 1.53.

20 This is perfectly plausible as history, but it also creates Moggaliputtatissa's mythos: by staying in the forest monastery frequented by the great meditation masters Śāṇavāsin and Upagupta, his charisma as a realized master is assured. He shows this spiritual power to Aśoka when he descends from the Ahogaṅga monastery. Aśoka is convinced that he is the only monk capable of stabilizing Buddhism, and hence invites Moggaliputtatissa to preside at the Third Council. In this way the spiritual charisma of the Mathuran forest lineage of Śāṇavāsin and Upagupta is crucial in enabling the purification of the Sangha and the establishment of the *vibhajjavāda*.

21 Obviously this was not, from a *vibhajjavādin* perspective, a schismatic community. At the time of the missions the Sangha of Mathura, whose Vinaya we now possess under the name of the Mūlasarvāstivāda, were clearly within the circle of the *vibhajjavādins*.

9.3 Soṇaka & Sāṇaka

22 It is even possible that Moggaliputtatissa shared ordination lineage with Śāṇavāsin. This possibility rests on the evident confusion between the similar names Soṇaka and Sāṇaka. The similarity is not merely phonetic. He is named after the robe he was accustomed to wear (*-vāsī*), which was either made of hemp cloth (*sāṇa-*), or was of red color (*soṇa-*).[25]

23 The Sinhalese Vinaya and Abhidhamma lineages mention a Soṇaka, one of the five early Vinaya masters: Upāli, Dāsaka, Soṇaka, Siggava, Moggaliputtatissa.[26] In the chronicles and commentaries the same list of Vinaya masters becomes partially fused with the account of the Councils, although the two are textually distinct.

24 Soṇaka must have lived at the same time as Śāṇavāsin, for they are both connected with the reign of Kāḷaśoka.[27] The Pali tradition says the Second

[25] Variation between these forms can occur even within different recensions of the same text. Thus MUKHOPADHYAYA'S edition of the Aśokāvadāna (on GRETIL) refers to Śāṇakavāsī, while the Nepalese manuscript of the same text has Soṇavāsī (according to MITRA, *Sanskrit Buddhist Literature*, pg. 10).

[26] This list is found in the late canonical Parivāra (5.1), where it begins an extended list of Vinaya masters encompassing several centuries of transmission in Sri Lanka.

[27] Dīpavaṁsa 4.52.

Council was held under Kāḷaśoka's patronage, and Śāṇavāsin participated in that Council according to all traditions, including the Pali.

25 This highlights a puzzling discrepancy: the Pali list of five Vinaya masters appears not to contain any of the Elders mentioned in the Second Council proceedings. It is really unthinkable that the most serious Vinaya crisis in Buddhist history, where monks gathered from all the Buddhist regions, should not have included a contemporary Vinaya master.

26 There are inescapable similarities between the Soṇaka found in the southern and the Śāṇavāsin of the northern sources.

Table 9.1: Parallels between Soṇaka & Śāṇavāsin

Soṇaka	Śāṇavāsin
Born in Kāsī, 45 AN	Born in Rājagaha, soon after Nirvana
Merchant's son	Merchant's son
When young, went on journey trading to Giribbaja (=Rājagaha).	When young, went on journey trading overseas
Goes to Veḷuvana at 15 years of age, with 55 companions	On return, goes to Veḷuvana
Sees Dāsaka, Upāli's student, and gains faith	Meets Ānanda and offers to hold 5-year festival
Goes forth with parents' permission, becomes an arahant versed in the Tipitaka	Goes forth, becomes arahant versed in the Tipitaka

27 I suggest that there were two separate narratives, one of the lineage of Elders, and one of the Second Council. In these, the same Elder might be known by different names. These separate passages were later fused, with the lineage of teachers preceding the Council narrative in some cases (Dīpavaṁsa, Mūlasarvāstivāda Vinaya). Thus in the Pali tradition the Soṇaka of the lineage becomes the Sambhūta Sāṇavāsin of the Second Council.

28 To corroborate this, the Mūlasarvāstivāda Vinaya is the only one of the Vinayas that directly combines the lineage of Elders with the Second Council. And there we find the name Śāṇaka[28] in the lineage, but *Yang-dag*

[28] 奢搦迦 (T24, № 1451, p. 411, b18). I cannot identify the exact form used for Śāṇavāsin in the Second Council, but it is certainly not the same. The nearest I can identify by

skyes (= Sambhūta) in the Second Council.[29] But this Sambhūta must be the Sambhūta Sāṇavāsin mentioned in the Pali. It is thus clear that both the Chinese and Tibetan versions of this Vinaya call the same Elder by different names in the two contexts.

29 Similarly, where the Samantapāsādikā, in comparing Moggaliputtatissa's work to the Theras of old, refers to Kassapa at the First Council and Yasa at the Second Council, the Sudassanavinayavibhāsā mentions Kassapa and Soṇaka.[30] This is immediately before a mention of the five Vinaya-masters, so must mean the same person, i.e. Śāṇavāsin = Soṇaka. In the account of the Second Council itself, however, we find 婆那參復多 (*po-na can-fu-tuo*),[31] for Sāṇasambhūta or Sonasambhūta.

30 There is, therefore, good reason to think a similar confusion has happened in the Pali tradition, and that Soṇaka is really Sāṇavāsin.

31 Now, Soṇaka/Śāṇavāsin is of course the preceptor of Upagupta; but he is also the preceptor of Siggava,[32] who in turn is Moggaliputtatissa's preceptor.[33] Thus, if our idea is correct, Moggaliputtatissa inherited the same ordination lineage as the Mūlasarvāstivādins of Mathura.

---

comparison with Rockhill's Tibetan rendering it should be 善見 (T24, № 1451, p. 413, b19), but this is rather Sudassana.

[29] ROCKHILL, 170, 176.

[30] 須那拘 (T24, № 1462, p. 684, b13). In the first mention of the Vinaya masters it is spelt 蘇那拘 (T24, № 1462, p. 677, b19–20).

[31] T24, № 1462, p. 678, a24.

[32] Samantapāsādikā 1.235: *Upālitthero sammāsambuddhassa santike uggaṇhi, dāsakatthero attano upajjhāyassa upālittherassa, soṇakatthero attano upajjhāyassa dāsakattherassa, siggavatthero attano upajjhāyassa soṇakattherassa, moggaliputtatissatthero attano upajjhāyassa siggavattherassa caṇḍavajjittherassa cāti.*
Sudassanavinayavibhāsā: 陀寫俱從優波離受。須提那俱從陀寫俱受。悉伽婆從須那俱受。目揵連子帝須從悉伽婆受。又栴陀跋受。如是師師相承乃至于今
(T24, № 1462, p. 716, c26–29).

[33] The story of Siggava, in response to a prophecy, intentionally visting Moggaliputtatissa's parents' house for alms for seven years before finding success closely echoes the story of Śāṇavāsin, in response to a prophecy, visting Upagupta's family home for many years before finding success.

9.4 The dragons of Kaśmīr

32 Those scholars who are not prepared to accept the Mathuran origins of the Mūlasarvāstivāda usually look to to the Northwest, especially Kaśmīr, for the home of this school. In this case we need to return to the missions accounts for information.

33 After the settling of the problems in the Sangha at the Third Council, Moggaliputtatissa decides that Buddhism would become well established in the border regions, and sends out missionaries across India. One of these is Majjhantika, who is sent to Kaśmīr, where he subdues a host of dragons and establishes the Dhamma. Dīpavaṁsa 7.3 sums up:

34 > 'Majjhantika the great sage, having gone to Gandhāra,
> Inspired the ferocious dragon and freed many from bondage.'

35 This Majjhantika is not regarded in any way as heretical. In fact he is the ordination teacher of Mahinda, the revered founder of Sinhalese Buddhism. This is mentioned in the commentarial accounts, and confirmed in the Dīpavaṁsa.[34] While the missionary story is, in general, mainly known from the southern sources, in this case there is one Chinese text that says that Majjhantika and Mahinda were told by Ānanda himself to go to, respectively, Kaśmīr and Sri Lanka.[35] In addition the Mahākarmavibhaṅga, describing missionary work by arahants of the Buddha's day, mentions Madhyandina subduing the dragons of Kaśmīr, and Mahendra overcoming of the Rakṣasas of Siṁhaladvīpa.[36] Thus the northern and southern sources are in perfect agreement.

36 Kaśmīr became the main centre for the Sarvāstivādins, so the story of Majjhantika recurs throughout the Sarvāstivādin influenced literature, including the Aśokarājasūtra,[37] Mūlasarvāstivādin Vinaya,[38] etc. There is evidently a problem in seeing a patriarch of the Sarvāstivādins as one of the fathers of the Mahāvihāravāsin school.

---

[34] Dīpavaṁsa 6.25: *Tato mahido pabbajito moggaliputtassa santike/Pabbājesi mahādevo majdhanto upasampade.*

[35] T № 1507, p.37, b16–27; see LAMOTTE, *History of Indian Buddhism*, 303.

[36] The Pali sources agree that old Sri Lanka was overrun by demons, e.g. Dīpavaṁsa 1.20.

[37] T № 2043; see RONGXI, 122–124.

[38] ROCKHILL, 167–170.

37 Thus Wynne[39] suggests Majjhantika was a follower of the *vibhajjavāda* who converted to Sarvāstivāda after arrival in Kaśmīr. But this scenario depends on the underlying assumption that *sarvāstivāda* and *vibhajjavāda* are opposing schools. In fact, there is no reason why Majjhantika should not have held opinions which we know of as *sarvāstivādin* while still in Pāṭaliputta, but these were not felt at the time to lie outside the spectrum of acceptable views; or perhaps he had no decided view on that point at that time; or perhaps he never held *sarvāstivādin* views but was tolerant of his followers who did; and so on. The point is that we don't have to think in terms of mutually opposing schools in such a complex and fluid situation.

38 The internal evidence of the Sarvāstivādins themselves suggests that the 'all exists' (*sarvam asti*) doctrine emerged after the Aśokan period. There is a famous passage, found throughout the Sarvāstivādin texts,[40] containing a well known list of teachers giving their views on the 'all exists' doctrine. Frauwallner notes that all the views in this passage differ from the mature position of the school, and the passage seems to be included in the Vibhāṣā as a 'doxographical appendix'. Thus it would seem to pre-date the compilation of the Vibhāṣā. It mentions the following teachers: Dharmatrāta, Ghoṣaka, Vasumitra, Buddhadeva. Bhavya, after presenting his three lists of schools, suggests, as another explanation of the schisms, that the arising of the schools was due to the diversity of opinions by these masters.[41] It seems we must regard these teachers as the developers of the 'all exists' doctrine, and none of them appear in the names we find mentioned in the Mauryan period.

39 This is confirmed in the San Lun Xuan Yi, a treatise written by Jia-xiang. In accounting for the appearance of the Mahāsaṅghikas he follows the account of the Mahāvibhāṣā. When it comes to the Sthaviras, he says that in the first 200 years there was the succession of teachers: Kassapa, Ānanda, Majjhantika, Śāṇavāsin, Upagupta, Pūrṇa, Mecaka, Kātyāyanīputra. From Kassapa to Mecaka was 200 years, during which period there was no schism.[42] At the beginning of the third century, Kātyāyanīputra passed away, and there was a split into two schools, Sthaviras and Sarvās-

---

[39] WYNNE, 32.

[40] See FRAUWALLNER, *Studies in Abhidharma Literature*, 185*ff*. for references and discussion.

[41] ROCKHILL, 194–5.

[42] 從迦葉至寐者柯二百年已來無異部 (T45, № 1852, p. 9, b20–21).

tivādins. Since Pūrṇa, there had been a gradual drifting away from the essentials, especially an excessive promotion of Abhidhamma over the Suttas. To escape the controversy, the Sthaviras went to the Himalayan region, and henceforth were called the Haimavatas.[43]

This account matches well with the picture we have drawn from the Pali sources. Both Moggaliputtatissa and Pūrṇa are separated from the Second Council by one 'generation' in the lineages, which puts them as approximate contemporaries around the time of Aśoka. The connection between Moggaliputtatissa and the Abhidhamma is central to his identity: not only does he compose the core of the Kathāvatthu, but his first interest in investigating Buddhism is sparked by hearing a cryptic Abhidhamma phrase from the Cittayamaka, described as the 'Buddhamantra'. So around the time of Aśoka these monks were participating in the formal investigation, classification, and clarification of the teachings from the Suttas. But only a couple of generations later, after the time of Kātyāyanīputra, did this result in a schism. This description of a long period of gestation and discussion, eventually resulting in division, is far more plausible than the more radical accounts of instant schism.

[43] T45, № 1852, p. 9, b15–c1.

CONCLUSION

WE CAN NO LONGER THINK OF 'PRE-SECTARIAN' AND 'SECTARIAN' Buddhism as two clear cut periods. Rather, there was an evolutionary process, whose complexity we can only guess at, and which we can know of only through fragments. Sectarian tendencies proceeded differently in different places. Just as Moggaliputtatissa escaped the conflicts by running off to retreat, so must many monastics have viewed the arguments as worldly Dhamma. Even Xuan-zang, a millenium after the Buddha, recorded many monks who did not belong to a school. Yet this should not blind us to the achievements of the sects: the development of sectarian organization made it possible to maintain the scriptures and keep the Dhamma alive.

2 Here is an interpretation of how early Buddhist sectarianism evolved.

3 **0–100 AN—Integrated Pre-sectarian Buddhism:** After the Parinibbana, the Buddhist community was in a state of uncertainty, even shock. It was imperative that they work together to make real the Buddha's injunction to take the Dhamma and Vinaya as their refuge. The hugeness of the task and the uncertainty of the future gave the Sangha ample reason to stick together, as a still untried fledgling spiritual movement.

4 **100–200 AN—Disintegrating Pre-sectarian Buddhism:** The very success of the Sangha in preserving itself and the Dhamma must inevitably breed complacency. The Second Council saw a significant rift over Vinaya practice, and it was only with difficulty that enough monks were assembled from the various districts to resolve the problem as a unified Sangha. The Aśokan period saw various divisive potentials within the Sangha rapidly multiply in potency. No longer could the Sangha deal with problems using its internal mechanisms, but had to rely on government support.

5 **200–300 AN—Emerging Sectarian Buddhism:** Spread out over vast areas, the Sangha evolved distinct regional identities. Local saints articulated more sophisticated and precise Abhidhammas. Lavish support enabled the establishment of local centers based around worship of stupas and relics, including those of the local saints. Texts became more firmly fixed in particular dialects. In the stupas of Vedisa many of these elements have emerged, but the community did not regard itself as a distinct 'school'.

6 **300+ AN—Sectarian Buddhism:** The constellation of sectarian tendencies was by now set irreversibly in the firmament. The emergence of sects, if it had not taken place already, was at hand. From now on the different communities saw themselves as irreversibly separate. The boundaries between the sects would never have been absolute, but they were there, and they played a crucial role in all subsequent developments.

7 I have followed the suggestions of earlier researchers in closely associating the emergence of schools with the Aśokan missionaries. But we do not know whether the leaders of the missions promulgated the doctrines of the schools. We must avoid the fallacy of back-reading a later situation into earlier times: 'sectarian tendency' or 'sectarian precursor' does not mean 'sect'.

8 None of the evidence for 'sudden schisms' in the Aśokan or pre-Aśokan period stands up to scrutiny. The sectarian accounts in which these ideas are found are mythic texts whose prime purpose is to authenticate the schools. The schools which flourished in the border regions tried to prove that they were the true bastion of real Buddhism. They did this by developing myths of origins. The Mahāvihāravāsins and Sarvāstivādins in particular felt the need to combine this mythic authority with a shrill denunciation of the 'opposing' sects. This reflects a lack of confidence and maturity of these schools in that period, and survives as evidence of a certain bitterness in local sectarian rivalries.

9 And yet even the most polemicized passages from the Mahāvibhāṣā confirm that the 'schisms' were not literal Vinaya schisms of the 'go-straight-to-hell' variety. There is no evidence anywhere for the formation of schools due to schisms in the narrow Vinaya sense, and much evidence against.

10 The mythic accounts of sect formation must, as historical documents, bow and exit before the 'Unity Edicts' of Aśoka himself. Using mythic texts

to decide whether the schism was in 116 AN or 137 AN is as sensible as using the Bible to decide whether the world was created in 4004 BCE. Aśoka said the Sangha was unified, and we have no reason to doubt him.

11 My findings constitute a radical departure from previous visionings of this period. If there is any merit in this analysis, we must rethink many of our ideas about how Buddhism formed. Not the least of the problems is the question of the interrelationship between the existing early canonical texts. These are usually held to stem primarily from the pre-sectarian period, then finalized and edited in the early sectarian period. Thus collating the corresponding parts of the different collections may take us back to before the schism. Shifting the root schism one or two centuries later could make a major difference in how these texts are dated.

12 I would note, though, that sectarian separation is only one factor to be taken into consideration. The accidents of history have decreed that the early canonical texts that have come down to us hail mainly from two areas: Sri Lanka and Kaśmīr/Gandhāra. These areas, 3000 kilometers apart, were established at the extreme ends of the Indic cultural sphere from the time of Aśoka. Even if the texts were not separated on sectarian grounds until later, this geographic separation must have meant the collections remained primarily isolated from this time. Thus collating the collections would still bear the promise of restoring us to the pre-Aśokan period.

13 All I have said so far is, of course, just stories of the past. Like any historian, in analyzing the myths of the past I am creating my own mythology, a mythology cast in the methods and concepts of the present. History lies to the extent that it pretends to have rejected myth, and has meaning to the extent that it owns up to its agenda: recreating the present in the image of the past. This is why history is so intensely political, and the act of pretending objectivity is just another political manouver. After many years of reading and contemplating both history and myth, I have come to believe that the main difference between the two is that myth has miracles, while history has footnotes.

Appendix A

CHRONOLOGY

DATING OF BUDDHIST EVENTS is a painfully complex and doubtful matter. Modern scholars early settled on *circa* 486 BCE as the date of the Buddha's parinibbana. This is based on a corrected reading of the Sinhalese sources and is known as the 'long chronology'. More recently, scholars proposed a 'short chronology' based on northern sources, placing the Buddha's Nibbana around 368 BCE. But the latest research is moving towards a 'median chronology' (the 'Rhys Davids/Gombrich theory'[1]), placing the Nibbana around 410 BCE, with a margin of error of 10–20 years either side. This is the dating I follow for this essay. To avoid the ambiguities associated with this calendar dating, however, it is often useful to compare events in terms of how long they happened 'After Nibbana', in which case the abbreviation AN is used. The following table is an attempt to *approximately* correlate the major events and persons in this work with the median chronology. I have based most of these dates on Cousins.[2]

2 Cousins and Gombrich bring the Second Council down to 60–80 AN. One reason for this is that some of the Elders at the Second Council are said to be students of Ānanda, and it is felt the gap between the Parinibbana and the Second Council is too great to be bridged by just one generation. But Ānanda was probably about 45 at the time of the Parinibbana, and may well have lived for another 40 years or so. Both the Pali and the

[1] COUSINS, 'The Dating of the Historical Buddha: A Review Article', 109.
[2] COUSINS, 'The "Five Points" and the Origins of the Buddhist Schools', 76.

northern traditions[3] contain statements to this effect. Given his character, it would be surprising if he were not still accepting students until his old age. A 20 year old student in 40 AN would be 80 at the traditional time of the Second Council. It would be unremarkable, if not probable, that this Council consisting of Elder bhikkhus, including the 'oldest monk on earth', should include monks of this age who had been ordained in Ānanda's day. Hence I see no reason to change the date of the Second Council. This means the Council could have been before or after Candragupta's ascension.

3 Vasumitra's schism date is given twice, according to whether we consider this by the calendar date in the text, or whether we correlate it with Aśoka's reign. The San-Lun-Xian-Yi (三論玄義, T45, № 1852, p. 9, b20–21) is a Sthaviran treatise composed by Jia-xiang between 397–419.

[3] T45, № 1852, p10, a08.

Table A.1: Chronology of Early Buddhism

	Median Chronology **BCE**	 **AN**	**Mahāvihāra Elders**	**San-Lun-Xian-Yi**	**Schism Accounts**
Original Buddhism	**458** Awakening		Upāli	Kassapa Ānanda	
Integrated Presectarian Buddhism	**413** Parinibbāna	**1** 1st Council (Rājagaha)	Dāsaka	Majjhantika	
	326 Alexander				
Dispersing Presectarian Buddhism	**313** Candragupta	**100** 2nd Council (Vesālī)	Soṇaka (Śāṇavāsin)	Śāṇavāsin	**100** Dīpavaṁsa Vasumitra
			Siggava	Upagupta	**137** Bhavya III
Emerging Sectarian Buddhism	**277–246** Aśoka	**154** 3rd Council (Pāṭaliputta)	Moggali- puttatissa		Vasumitra
			Mahinda	Pūrṇa	
Sectarian Buddhism	**185–151** Puṣyamitra		(Hemavata teachers) (Gotiputa)	Mecaka **(200 AN)** Kātyāyanī- putra	Śāriputra- paripṛcchā

Appendix B

ASOKA & THE FIRST SCHISM

EVERY ANALYSIS OF THE SCHISMS that I have read by modern scholars places the schisms before Aśoka. Thus Bechert says, speaking of the Third Council: 'After the individual Sanghas (of whom many had been divided as a result of *saṅghabheda*, i.e. "splitting of the Order" or "schism") were re-united in this manner'.[1] But the Third Council narrative says nothing about the existence of several distinct 'Sanghas'. Again, Bechert says: 'the first schism, which must be placed before Aśoka'.[2] Prebish concurs: 'Now we all know that a schism did take place around this time.'[3] And Cousins also agrees: 'Even if it is now clear that the schism between the Mahāsaṅghikas and the Sthaviravāda is not connected with the Second Council, it cannot have been long after.'[4]

2 Nevertheless, I think this event must be placed after Aśoka. Such a mass of authority cannot be discarded lightly, and I should explain why I have come to different conclusions. Strangely enough, I have never come across an explicit argument for exactly why the root schism must be pre-Aśokan, but the reasoning must go something like this.

3 The texts as we have them ascribe the schisms to one of three periods relative to Aśoka: before (Dīpavaṁsa and Bhavya III), during (Vasumitra and probably the Sarvāstivāda generally), or after (Śāriputraparipṛcchā).

---

1 BECHERT, 'Theravāda Buddhist Sangha', 3.
2 BECHERT, 'The Date of the Buddha Reconsidered', 66.
3 PREBISH, 'Review of Scholarship on Buddhist Councils', 237.
4 COUSINS, 'Pali Oral Literature', 104.

Two sources place the schisms before Aśoka. This includes the Sinhalese tradition, which is more historically reliable. Vasumitra places events in the time of Aśoka, but this is a short chronology text. The calendar date of the schism according to Vasumitra is about 100 AN. This roughly agrees in years with the Dīpavaṁsa (100+ AN) and Bhavya III (137 AN). Vasumitra, therefore, has the date approximately right, but following the tradition of his school, he thinks that this was the reign of Aśoka. Apparently this tradition confuses the Vajjian 'Kāḷaśoka' of the Second Council with the famous 'Dharmāśoka' of Magadha. The Śāriputraparipṛcchā is closely related to this tradition, but in placing the schism later has become confused in its chronology. The 'Schism edicts' indicate that either Aśoka was not fully aware of what was going on—which was sometimes the case[5]—or that he is referring to a mere party dispute among the Theravādins.

4 We have already demonstrated some problems with this reasoning. The Dīpavaṁsa should be entirely disregarded in this matter. Bhavya III is late, unsupported, and polemical. We know little of the Puggalavāda mythos, and so cannot interpret the meaning this story had for the school. But like all the other versions, it would have been constructed to legitimize the communal identity of the school.

5 Vasumitra is speaking in the same tradition as the Mahāvibhāṣā, and although the Mahāvibhāṣā does not mention the King's name, we should see these sources as representing the same mythos. The events happened under a pious Buddhist king of Pāṭaliputta who sponsored the Kaśmīr mission. The purpose of the myth is to associate the Sarvāstivādins of Kaśmīr with the root Sthaviras in the time of Aśoka. The calendar date is irrelevant to this mythos, and has merely been inserted to give historical fixity to an event which, from Vasumitra's point of view, must have happened around that time.

6 For similar reasons, we cannot discount the 'Unity Edicts' as being merely Aśoka's unawareness of what was happening in the Sangha. This argument creates an insoluble dilemma. The same texts that tell us that the schism was Aśokan or pre-Aśokan also assert Aśoka's intimate involvement in the schisms. It is Aśoka's involvement, not the date, that is the key

---

[5] For example, the Kandahar Edicts say that the fishers and hunters had stopped fishing and hunting, which according to Basham is sheer complacency (BASHAM, 59).

issue. The date merely fixes the events in line with the general chronology of the different schools. So are we to discard the critical element of Aśokan involvement while accepting the incidental detail of the date? Of course it is quite possible that Aśoka was not fully aware of what was happening, but if he was unaware, the sources are unreliable.

7 And regarding the supposed 'confusion' of the Śāriputrapariprcchā, we can only assert that, aside from its obvious mythical nature and several textual problems, it is not confused about its own chronology. The ascription of the schism to a date after Aśoka is no accident, but is inherent in the logic of the text. First it acknowledges the usual five 'Masters of the Law', culminating with Upagupta, who is contemporary with Aśoka. Clearly there is no schism so far, as the list of patriarchs is identical with the mainstream (Mūla) Sarvāstivāda tradition. After Aśoka we are told of the persecutions under Puṣyamitra; again, this is entirely in accord with the (Mūla) Sarvāstivāda tradition.[6] The events of the root schism itself are very different from the other accounts, and so while the account of the '18 schools' shares a common basis with Vasumitra, we cannot infer that the account of the root schism is merely a confusion of Vasumitra.

8 Lamotte says that this text is: 'so obscure that it allows for the most diverse interpretations. After having narrated at length the persecution by the Śuṅga Puṣyamitra, the text, going back to the past, speaks of events which took place under a king whom it does not name, but who, from the evidence of other parallel texts which we shall quote, can be none other than Aśoka the Maurya.'[7] But the text, in this respect at least, is not at all obscure, nor does it hint at a flashback in time, but simply relates a series of consecutive events. I agree with Lamotte that Fa-xiang's version of events in his postface to the Mahāsaṅghika Vinaya is related to the Śāriputrapariprcchā, but it is Fa-xiang who, writing at a much later date, has got the chronology confused. He too starts with an evil king who persecutes the bhikkhus; but this must be Puṣyamitra, as there are no known pre-Aśokan persecutions. Then he goes on to relate the story of the king

---

[6] For various versions of this legend, see LAMOTTE, *History of Indian Buddhism*, 386–392.

[7] LAMOTTE, *History of Indian Buddhism*, 172.

presiding over the vote with tally-sticks; but to the Śāriputraparipṛcchā's account he adds the anachronistic detail that the king was Aśoka.[8]

9 The first calendar date the text gives us is 300 AN for the division of the root Sthaviras into Sarvāstivāda and Puggalavāda. In the text's short chronology, this would be roughly 170 years after Aśoka's death, which again makes perfect sense of the internal chronology. The Mahāsaṅghika schisms, as is generally the case, are said to be earlier than the Sthavira schisms, so they are dated 200 AN. This brings them, say, 70 years after Aśoka, around 170 BCE. Puṣyamitra died around 151 BCE, so our dates are about 20 years out. But given that the Śāriputraparipṛcchā speaks in units no smaller than centuries, who's to worry about a few decades here and there? In any case, this relates to a later portion of the text. Thus we can definitely conclude that the internal chronology of the relevant portions of the Śāriputraparipṛcchā is not confused. It merely disagrees with the chronology of other texts.

10 Can we say anything else about the chronology of the Śāriputraparipṛcchā? One relevant detail is the interference of the King. This agrees with the Mahāsaṅghika Vinaya. But the Mahāvihāravāsin Vinaya says nothing about royal interference, despite the school's approval, even celebration, of Aśoka's interference as establishing the essential model for Sangha/State relations, thus ensuring the very survival of the Dhamma. Of course the later Mahāvihāravāsin texts assert that Kāḷasoka sponsored the Second Council and Ajātasattu sponsored the first, but these are just back-readings to authorize Aśoka's role. Such justifications for Royal involvement, while not against the general spirit of Indian legal procedures, must be post-Aśokan.[9] Similarly, the use of tally-sticks to vote in an important procedure is not supported by the Pali Vinaya, although we should not be surprised if the Mahāsaṅghika Vinaya took a different perspective on this. Finally, we note the mention of written texts, which likewise place the text no earlier than the post-Aśokan period.

11 One of the most pervasive motivations in forming mythic texts is to seek archaic authorization for contemporary events, hence the very common

---

[8] LAMOTTE, *History of Indian Buddhism*, 173.

[9] The lack of mention of Aśoka and royal interference in Sangha affairs is, incidentally, one of the reasons for thinking the Pali Vinaya was fixed relatively early.

mythic tendency to date formative events earlier rather than later. Therefore, the version placing the schism later is likely to be more reasonable. In addition, the Śāriputraparipṛcchā is less polemical than the other versions, indicating a healthier and more realistic attitude towards such things, and consequently fewer motives to twist events to its own perspective. We have also seen that this version is in perfect accord with the epigraphic evidence and with the Mahāvihāra Vinaya commentaries.

BIBLIOGRAPHY

For the Pali I used the Vipassana Research Institute text, with the exception of the Dīpavaṁsa, which I retrieved from GRETIL.

ALLCHIN, F.R. *The Archaeology of Early Historic South Asia.* Cambridge University Press, 2004.

ALLON, Mark. *Style and Function.* Tokyo: International College for Advanced Buddhist Studies, 1997.

———. *The Mahāparinirvāṇa Sūtra.* (unpublished Honors submission), 1987.

ANĀLAYO. 'The Buddha and Omniscience.' Indian International Journal of Buddhist Studies 7, 2006.

AUNG, Shwe Zan and C.A.F. RHYS DAVIDS. *Points of Controversy.* Oxford: Pali Text Society, 2001.

BANDARANAYAKE, Senake. *The pre-modern city in Sri Lanka: the "first" and "second" urbanization.*
www.arkeologi.uu.se/digitalAssets/9/9377_bandaranayake.pdf

BAPAT, P.V. and HIRAKAWA, A. *Shan-Chien-P'i-P'o-Sha: A Chinese version by Sanghabhadra of Samantapāsādikā.* Poona: Bhandarkar Oriental Research Institute, 1970.

BAPAT, P.V. *2500 Years Of Buddhism.*
http://www.quangduc.com/English/history/032500years01.html

BARUA, Dwijendra Lal. 'A Few Evidences on the Age of the Kathavatthu'. The Indian Historical Quarterly, № 2, 1937. 367–370.

BASHAM, A.L. 'Aśoka and Buddhism: a re-examination.' *Buddhism: Critical Concepts in Religious Studies.* Ed. Paul WILLIAMS. Vol I. Routledge, 2005. 54–63.

BASTOW, David. 'The First Argument for Sarvāstivāda'. Asian Philosophy, Vol 5.2, 2/10/1995. 109–125.
http://ccbs.ntu.edu.tw/FULLTEXT/JR-ADM/Bastow.htm

BEAL, Samuel. *Buddhist Records of the Western World.* New Delhi: Oriental Book Reprint Corporation, 1983.

———. 'The Eighteen Schools of Buddhism (by Vasumitra).' The Indian Antiquary. V^OL 9. Bombay: Education Society's Press, 1880. 299*ff.*

BECHERT, Heinz. 'Notes on the Formation of Buddhist Sects and the Origins of Mahāyāna.' *Buddhism: Critical Concepts in Religious Studies.* Ed. Paul WILLIAMS. V^OL II. London: Routledge, 2005. 23–33.

———. 'The Date of the Buddha Reconsidered.' *Buddhism: Critical Concepts in Religious Studies.* Ed. Paul WILLIAMS. V^OL II. London: Routledge, 2005. 64–71.

———. 'Theravāda Buddhist Saṅgha.' *Buddhism: Critical Concepts in Religious Studies.* Ed. Paul WILLIAMS. V^OL II. London: Routledge, 2005. 1–22.

BINGENHEIMER, Marcus. *Der Monchsgelehrte Yinshun (*1906) und seine Bedeutung fur den Chinesisch-Taiwanischen Buddhismus im 20.* Jahrhundert. Heidelberg: Wurzburger Sinologische Schriften, 2004.

BIZOT, François. *Les traditions de la pabbajjaa en Asie du Sud-Est: Recherches sur le bouddhisme khmer IV.* Göttingen: Vandenhoeck & Ruprecht, 1988.

BODHI, Bhikkhu. *The Connected Discourses of the Buddha.* Somerville: Wisdom Publications, 2000.

———. *The Discourse on the All-embracing Net of Views.* Kandy: Buddhist Publication Society, 1978.

BUDDHAGHOSA. Trans. Bhikkhu ÑĀṆAMOḶI. *The Path of Purification.* Kandy: Buddhist Publication Society.

CHÂU, Bhikshu Thích Thiện. *The Literature of the Personalists of Early Buddhism.* Delhi: Motilal Barnasidass, 1996.

CHOONG, Mun-keat (Wei-keat). 'A Discussion on the Determination of the Date of the Historical Buddha'. Journal of Indian History, 1997–1999. V^OL lxxvi–lxxvii. http://ccbs.ntu.edu.tw/FULLTEXT/JR-MISC/misc115791.htm

CLARKE, Shayne. 'Vinaya Matṛkā—Mother of the Monastic Codes or Just Another Set of Lists?' Indo-Iranian Journal, 2004. 77–120.

———. 'Miscellaneous Musings on Mūlasarvāstivāda Monks'. Japanese Journal of Religious Studies 33/1, 2006. 1–49.

COLLINS, Steven. 'On the Very Idea of the Pali Canon.' *Buddhism: Critical Concepts in Religious Studies.* Ed. Paul WILLIAMS. V^OL I. London: Routledge, 2005. 72–95.

COUSINS, L.S. 'Buddhist Jhāna: its nature and attainment according to the Pali sources.' *Buddhism: Critical Concepts in Religious Studies.* Ed. Paul WILLIAMS. V^OL II. London: Routledge, 2005. 34–51.

———. 'On the Vibhajjavādins.' Buddhist Studies Review 18.2, 2001. 131–182.

———. 'Pali Oral Literature.' *Buddhism: Critical Concepts in Religious Studies.* Ed. Paul WILLIAMS. V^OL I. London: Routledge, 2005. 96–104.

———. 'Person and Self.' *Buddhism: Critical Concepts in Religious Studies.* Ed. Paul WILLIAMS. V^OL II. London: Routledge, 2005. 84–101.

———. 'The Dating of the Historical Buddha: A Review Article.' Journal of the Royal Asiatic Society 3.6.1, 1996. 57–63.

———. 'The "Five Points" and the Origins of the Buddhist Schools.' *Buddhism: Critical Concepts in Religious Studies*. Ed. Paul WILLIAMS. V^OL II. London: Routledge, 2005. 52–83.

DUTT, Nalinaksha. *Buddhism in Kashmir*. Delhi: Eastern Book Linkers, 1985.

———. *Buddhist Sects in India*. New Delhi: Motilal Banarsidass, 1998.

EDGERTON, Franklin. *Buddhist Hybrid Sanskrit Grammar and Dictionary*. Delhi: Motilal Barnasidass, 2004.

ENOMOTO, Fumio. 'Mūlasarvāstivādin and Sarvāstivādin.' Christine CHAJNACKI, Jens-Uwe HARTMANN, and Volker M. TSCHANNERL. Vividharatnakarandaka Festgabe fur Adelheid Mette. Swisstal-Odendorf, 2000.

FOGELIN, Lars. *Archaeology of Early Buddhism*. Oxford: Altamira Press, 2006.

FRAUWALLNER, E. *Studies in Abhidharma Literature*. Albany: State University of New York Press, 1995.

———. *The Earliest Vinaya and the Beginnings of Buddhist Literature*. Istituto Italiano per il Medio ed Estremo Oriente, 1956.

GOMBRICH, R.F. 'Recovering the Buddha's Message.' *Buddhism: Critical Concepts in Religious Studies*. Ed. Paul WILLIAMS. V^OL I. London: Routledge, 2005. 113–128.

GURUGE, Ananda W.P. 'Shan-Jian-Lu-Piposha as an authentic source on the early history of Buddhism and Aśoka.' *Dhamma-Vinaya: Essays in Honor of Venerable Professor Dhammavihari (Jotiya Dhirasekera)*. Ed. Asanga GURUGE, Toschiichi ENDO, G.A. SOMARATNE, and Sanath NANAYAKKARA. Sri Lanka Association for Buddhist Studies (SLABS), 2005. 92–110.

HALLISEY, Charles. 'Councils as Ideas and Events in the Theravada.' *Buddhism: Critical Concepts in Religious Studies*. Ed. Paul WILLIAMS. V^OL II. London: Routledge, 2005. 171–185.

HEIRMANN, Ann. 'Can We Trace the Early Dharmaguptakas?', 2002. www.brill.nl

———. *Rules for Nuns According to the Dharmaguptakavinaya*. Delhi: Motilal Barnasidass, 2002.

HEIRMANN, A.M. 'Buddha and Devadatta.' Indian Antiquary, V^OL 52, October 1923. 267–72. V^OL 54, October 1925. 98–99. http://ccbs.ntu.edu.tw/FULLTEXT/JR-ENG/hocbud.htm

HIRAKAWA, Akira. *A History of Indian Buddhism*. Delhi: Motilal Barnasidass, 1998.

HOPKINS, Jeffrey. *Meditation on Emptiness*. London: Wisdom Publications, 1983.

I-TSING. *A Record of the Buddhist Religion as Practiced in India and the Malay Archipelago*. Trans. J. TAKAKUSU. Delhi: Asian Educational Services, 2005.

JAYAWICKRAMA, N.A. *The Inception of Discipline and Vinaya Nidāna*. London: Pali Text Society, 1986.

JOHNSTON, E.H. *Aśvaghoṣa's Buddhacarita or Acts of the Buddha*. Delhi: Motilal Barnasidass, 2004.

LAMOTTE, Étienne. *History of Indian Buddhism*. Paris: Peeters Press, 1976.

———. 'The Assessment of Textual Authenticity in Buddhism.' *Buddhism: Critical Concepts in Religious Studies*. Ed. Paul WILLIAMS. V^OL I. London: Routledge, 2005. 192.

LAW, Bimala Churn. *The Debates Commentary*. Oxford: Pali Text Society, 1940, reprinted 1999.

———. 'Chronology of the Pali Canon'. Annals of the Bhandarkar Oriental Research Institute, Poona. 171–201.

LEGGE, James. *A Record of Buddhistic Kingdoms*. Delhi: Munshiram Manoharlal, 1998.

LENZ, Timothy. *A New Version of the Gandhari Dharmapada and a Collection of Previous-Birth Stories*. Seattle and London: University of Washington Press, 2003.

LIANG, Tao-wei. 'A Study on the I-Pu-Tsung-Lun.' Hua-Kang Buddhist Journal, № 02. Taipei: The Chung-Hwa Institute of Buddhist Studies, 1972. 25–65. http://www.chibs.edu.tw/publication/hkbj/02/hkbj0208.htm

MCEVILLEY, Thomas. *The Shape of Ancient Thought*. New York: Allworth Press, 2002.

MCQUEEN, Graeme. *A Study of the Śrāmanyaphala-Sūtra*. Wiesbaden: Otto Harrassowitz, 1988.

MITRA, Kalipada. 'Cross-cousin Relation Between Buddha and Devadatta.' http://ccbs.ntu.edu.tw/FULLTEXT/JR-ENG/kal.htm

MITRA, R.L. *The Lalita Vistara*. Delhi: Sri Satguru Publications, 1998.

———. *The Sanskrit Buddhist Literature of Nepal*. Asiatic Society of Bengal, 1882.

MONIER-WILLIAMS, M. *A Sanskrit-English Dictionary*. Delhi: Motilal Barnasidass, 2002.

MUKHERJEE, Biswadeb. 'The Riddle of the First Buddhist Council—A Retrospection.' Chung-Hwa Buddhist Journal, № 7, 1994. 452–473. http://ccbs.ntu.edu.tw/FULLTEXT/JR-BJ001/07_15.htm

MUKHOPADHYAYA, Sujitkumar. *The Aśokāvadāna*. Delhi: Sahitya Akademi, 1963.

NAKAMURA, Hajime. *Indian Buddhism*. Delhi: Motilal Barnasidass, 1996.

ÑĀṆAMOḶI, Bhikkhu and Bhikkhu BODHI. The Middle Length Discourses of the Buddha. Somerville: Wisdom Publications, 2005.

ÑĀṆAMOḶI, Bhikkhu. *The Patimokkha*. Bangkok: Mahamakutarajavidyalaya, 1969.

———. *The Path of Discrimination*. Oxford: Pali Text Society, 2002.

NATTIER, Jan and Charles S. PREBISH. 'Mahāsaṅghika Origins.' *Buddhism: Critical Concepts in Religious Studies*. Ed. Paul WILLIAMS. V^OL II. London: Routledge, 2005. 199–228.

NORMAN, K.R. *A Philological Approach to Buddhism*. London: School of Oriental and African Studies (University of London), 1997.

ÑĀṆASAṀVARA, Somdet. *Buddha Sāsana Vaṁsa.* Trans. Bhikkhu KANTASILO. Bangkok: Mahamakut Press, 1974.
PACHOW, W. *A Comparative Study of the Pratimoksa.* Delhi: Motilal Barnasidass, 2000.
PERERA, H.R. 'Buddhism in Sri Lanka: A short history.' http://buddhanet.net/ebooks_hist_art.htm
PREBISH, Charles S. *Buddhist Monastic Discipline.* Delhi: Motilal, 2002.
———. 'Review of Scholarship on Buddhist Councils.' *Buddhism: Critical Concepts in Religious Studies.* Ed. Paul WILLIAMS. V^OL^ I. London: Routledge, 2005. 224–243.
———. 'Śaikṣa-Dharmas Revisited.' *Buddhism: Critical Concepts in Religious Studies.* Ed. Paul WILLIAMS. V^OL^ II. London: Routledge, 2005. 186–198.
———. 'The Prātimokṣa Puzzle.' *Buddhism: Critical Concepts in Religious Studies.* Ed. Paul WILLIAMS. V^OL^ I. London: Routledge, 2005. 257–271.
———. 'Theories Concerning the Skandhaka.' *Buddhism: Critical Concepts in Religious Studies.* Ed. Paul WILLIAMS. V^OL^ I. London: Routledge, 2005. 244–256.
PURI, B.N. *Buddhism in Central Asia.* Delhi: Motilal Barnasidass, 2000.
RADICE, William. *Myths and Legends of India.* London: The Folio Society, 2001.
RAY, Reginald. 'A Condemned Saint: Devadatta.' www.leighb.com/Devadatta.pdf
REYNOLDS, Craig James. *The Buddhist Monkhood in Nineteenth Century Thailand.* Cornell University, 1972.
ROCKHILL, W. Woodville. *The Life of the Buddha.* New Delhi: Asian Educational Services, 1992.
RONGXI, Li, trans. *The Biographical Scripture of King Aśoka.* Berkeley: Numata Center for Buddhist Translation and Research, 1993.
ROTH, Gustav. *Bhikṣuṇī Vinaya.* Patna: K.P. Jayaswal Research Institute, 1970.
SALOMON, Richard. *Ancient Buddhist Scrolls from Gandhāra.* Seattle: University of Washington Press, 1999.
SARAO, K.T.S. 'In-laws of the Buddha as Depicted in Pāli Sources.' Chung-Hwa Buddhist Journal, № 17. Taipei: The Chung-Hwa Institute of Buddhist Studies, 2004. 243–265. http://www.chibs.edu.tw/publication/chbj/17/chbj1709.htm#nt15
SASAKI, Shizuka. 'Buddhist Sects in the Aśoka Period. (1) The Meaning of the Schism Edict.' Buddhist Studies (Bukkyo Kenkyu), V^OL^ 18. Hamamatsu: International Buddhist Association, 1989. 157–176.
———. 'Buddhist Sects in the Aśoka Period. (2) Saṁghabheda (1).' Buddhist Studies (Bukkyo Kenkyu), V^OL^ 21. Hamamatsu: International Buddhist Association, 1992. 157–176.
———. 'Buddhist Sects in the Aśoka Period. (3) Saṁghabheda (2).' Buddhist Studies (Bukkyo Kenkyu), V^OL^ 22. Hamamatsu: International Buddhist Association, 1993. 167–199.

———. 'Buddhist Sects in the Aśoka Period. (4) The Structure of the Mahāsaṅghika Vinaya.' Buddhist Studies (Bukkyo Kenkyu), Vol 23. Hamamatsu: International Buddhist Association, 1994. 55–100.

———. 'Buddhist Sects in the Aśoka Period. (5) Presenting a Hypothesis.' Buddhist Studies (Bukkyo Kenkyu), Vol 24. Hamamatsu: International Buddhist Association, 1995. 165–225.

———. 'Buddhist Sects in the Aśoka Period. (6) The Dīpavaṁsa.' Buddhist Studies (Bukkyo Kenkyu). Hamamatsu: International Buddhist Association, 1996. 29–63.

———. 'Buddhist Sects in the Aśoka Period. (7) The Vibhāṣā and the Śāriputraparipṛcchā.' Buddhist Studies (Bukkyo Kenkyu). Hamamatsu: International Buddhist Association, Vol 27, 1998. 1–55.

———. 'Buddhist Sects in the Aśoka Period. (8) Supplementary Argument.' Buddhist Studies (Bukkyo Kenkyu), Vol 28. Hamamatsu: International Buddhist Association, 1999. 1–10.

SCHOPEN, Gregory. *Bones, Stones, and Buddhist Monks.* Honolulu: University of Hawai'i Press, 1997.

———. *Buddhist Monks and Business Matters.* Honolulu: University of Hawai'i Press, 2004.

———. *Figments and Fragments of Mahāyāna Buddhism in India.* Honolulu: University of Hawai'i Press, 2005.

SEN, Jyotirmay. 'Aśoka's mission to Ceylon and some connected problems.' The Indian Historical Quarterly, 1928, Vol 4:4. 667–678.

SENEVIRATNE, Anuradha. 'King Aśoka and Buddhism', 1994. http://www.buddhanet.net/ebooks_hist_art.htm

SHARF, Robert H. 'Buddhist Modernism and the Rhetoric of Meditative Experience.' *Buddhism: Critical Concepts in Religious Studies.* Ed. Paul WILLIAMS. Vol II. London: Routledge, 2005. 255–299.

SHUN, Yin. 'The Establishment of Sautrāntika-Darṣṭāntika and their Sub-sects.' Journal of Buddhist Studies, May 2003. 238–270.

STRONG, John S. *The Legend and Cult of Upagupta.* Delhi: Motilal Barnasidass, 1994.

———. *The Legend of King Aśoka.* Delhi: Motilal Barnasidass, 2002.

SUJATO, Bhikkhu. *A History of Mindfulness.* Taipei: Corporate Body of the Buddha Educational Foundation, 2006. Santipada.

———. *A Swift Pair of Messengers.* Penang: Inward Path Publishers, 2001; Santipada 2011.

———. *White Bones Red Rot Black Snakes.* Santipada, 2011.

SUNG, Kan-yuan. 'Tradition and Development in the Mo-ho-seng-chi'i-lü'. MA thesis for University of Calgary, 1999. http://buddhism.lib.ntu.edu.tw/FULLTEXT/JR-ADM/adm93485-1.htm

SUZUKI, Teitaro. 'The First Buddhist Council', 1904.
http://www.sacred-texts.com/journals/mon/1stbudcn.htm

TĀRANĀTHA. *Tāranātha's History of Buddhism in India*. Ed. Debiprasad CHATTOPADHYAYA. Trans. Alaka CHATTOPADHYAYA and Lama CHIMPA. Delhi: Motilal Barnasidass, 2004.

TSOMO, Karma Lekshe. *Sisters in Solitude*. Albany: State University of New York Press, 1996.

VASUMITRA. Trans. S. BEAL. 'The Eighteen Schools of Buddhism', 1880.
http://www.sacred-texts.com/journals/ia/18sb.htm

WALSER, Joseph. *Nāgārjuna in Context*. New York: Columbia University Press, 2005.

WARDER, A.K. *Indian Buddhism*. Delhi: Motilal Barnasidass, 2004.

WARNER, Rex. *Encyclopedia of World Mythology*. London: Peerage Books, 1970.

WIJEBANDARA, Chandima. *Early Buddhism: Its Religious and Intellectual Milieu*. Colombo: University of Kelaniya, 1993.

WILLEMEN, Charles, Bart DESSEIN, Collet COX. *Sarvāstivāda Buddhist Scholasticism*. Leiden, New York, Koln: Brill, 1998.

WILLIS, Michael. 'Buddhist Saints in Ancient Vedisa.' Journal of the Royal Asiatic Society, 2001, Series 3.

WOOLNER, Alfred C. *Aśoka: Text and Glossary*. Delhi: Low Price Publishers, 1993.

WYNNE, Alexander. 'How Old is the Suttapitaka?' Oxford Center for Buddhist Studies, 2003.
http://www.ocbs.org/research.php